DEVELOPMENTAL EXERCISES

to accompany

THE LITTLE, BROWN COMPACT HANDBOOK
Fifth Edition

By Jane E. Aaron

Donna Gorrell
St. Cloud University

with additional exercises by
Kathryn Riley
University of Minnesota Duluth

PEARSON
Longman

New York Boston San Francisco
London Toronto Sydney Tokyo Singapore Madrid
Mexico City Munich Paris Cape Town Hong Kong Montreal

Developmental Exercises to accompany Aaron, *The Little, Brown Compact Handbook, Fifth Edition*

Copyright ©2004 Pearson Education, Inc.

All rights reserved. Printed in the United States of America. Instructors may reproduce portions of this book for classroom use only. All other reproductions are strictly prohibited without prior permission of the publisher, except in the case of brief quotations embodied in critical articles and reviews.

ISBN: 0-321-17291-4

1 2 3 4 5 6 7 8 9 10–ML–06 05 04 03

CONTENTS

To the Student..vii

CLARITY AND STYLE

1. Emphasis: Beginnings and endings (11b)..1
2. Emphasis: Coordinating equal ideas (11c)..2
3. Emphasis: Subordinating ideas (11d)...3
4. Emphasis: Effective subordination (11d)...4
5. Parallelism: With *and, but, or, nor, yet* (12a)..5
6. Parallelism: With *both..and, either...or*, etc.; with lists and outlines (12a,b)...........6
7. Variety and Details (13) 7
8. Appropriate and Exact Language: Appropriate language (14a).................................8
9. Appropriate and Exact Language: Biased language (14a) 9
10. Appropriate and Exact Language: Exact language (14b).......................................10
11. Appropriate and Exact Language: Idioms (14b)...11
12. Appropriate and Exact Language: Confusing language (14 and 41a)....................12
13. Conciseness: Focusing on subject and verb, cutting empty words and repetition, reducing clauses and phrases (16a,b,c,d)..13
14. Conciseness: using strong verbs and active voice, cutting *there is*, combining sentences, rewriting jargon (16a,e,f,g)...14

SENTENCE PARTS AND PATTERNS

Basic Grammar

15. Parts of Speech: Nouns, pronouns, verbs (17a,b,c) 15
16. Parts of Speech: Nouns and verbs (17a,c)...17
17. Parts of Speech: Adjectives and adverbs (17d) 19
18. Parts of Speech: Connecting words (17e)...20
19. The Sentence: Subject and predicate (18a) 21
20. The Sentence: Predicate patterns (18b)...22
21. Phrases and Subordinate Clauses: Phrases (19a) 24
22. Phrases and Subordinate Clauses: clauses (19b)..26
23. Sentence Types (20)...27

Verbs

24. Verb Forms: Irregular verbs (21a,b)..28
25. Verb Forms: -*s* and -*ed* forms (21c)...30
26. Verb Forms: Helping verbs (21d)..32
27. Verb Forms: Verb + gerund or infinitive (21e)...33
28. Verb Forms: Verb + particle (21f)...34
29. Verb Tenses: Present and perfect (22a,b)..35
30. Verb Tenses: Progressive (22c) 37
31. Verb Tenses: Consistency and sequence (22d,e)...38

32	Verb Tenses: Conditional sentences and indirect quotations (22e)	39
33	Mood Of Verbs: Subjunctive (23)	40
34	Voice Of Verbs: Active vs. passive (24)	41
35	Subject-Verb Agreement: Intervening words, inverted order, and linking verbs (25b,i,j)	42
36	Subject-Verb Agreement: Subjects with *and*; subjects with *or, nor* (25c,d)	44
37	Subject-Verb Agreement: Indefinite pronouns, collective nouns, singular nouns ending in-*S*, titles and defined words (25e,f,h,k)	45
38	Subject-Verb Agreement: *Who, which, that* (25g)	46
39	Subject-Verb Agreement: Review (25)	47
40	Irregular Verbs (21b)	48

Pronouns

41	Pronoun Case (26a,b,d)	49
42	Pronoun Case: *Who, whom* (26c)	51
43	Pronoun-Antecedent Agreement I (27)	52
44	Pronoun-Antecedent Agreement II (27)	53
45	Pronoun Reference I (28)	54
46	Pronoun Reference II (28)	55
47	Pronouns: Review (26, 27, 28)	56

Modifiers

48	Adjectives and Adverbs (29)	57
49	Adjectives (29)	58
50	Order of Adjectives I (29, 30a)	59
51	Order of Adjectives II (29, 30a)	60
52	Adjectives and Adverbs: Determiners (29f)	61
53	Adjectives and Adverbs: Present and past participles (29e)	62
54	Misplaced Modifiers (30a)	63
55	Dangling Modifiers (30b)	64

Sentence Faults

56	Fragments I (31)	65
57	Fragments II (31)	66
58	Comma Splices and Fused Sentences: *and, but*, etc. (32a)	67
59	Comma Splices and Fused Sentences: *however*, etc. (32b)	68
60	Comma Splices And Fused Sentences: Review (32)	69
61	Mixed Sentences (33a,b)	70
62	Mixed Sentences: Repeated subjects and other parts (33c)	71

PUNCTUATION

63	End Punctuation (34)	72
64	Comma: With coordinating conjunctions and introductory elements (35a,b)	73
65	Comma: With nonessential elements (35c)	75

66	Comma: With items in series; two or more adjectives; dates, addresses, place names, long numbers; *she said*, etc. (35d,e,f,g)	76
67	Comma: Misuses (35h)	77
68	Comma: Review (35)	78
69	Semicolon (36)	79
70	Semicolon: Misuses (36d)	80
71	Colon (37)	81
72	Apostrophe: Possessive Case (38a)	82
73	Apostrophe: Contractions (38c)	83
74	Apostrophes (38)	84
75	Apostrophe: Review (38)	85
76	Punctuation Review: Apostrophes and Hyphens (38, 42)	87
77	Quotation Marks I (39)	88
78	Quotation Marks or Underlining (39, 44a)	89
79	Quotation Marks II (39)	90
80	Dash, Parentheses, Ellipsis Mark, Brackets, Slash (40)	91
81	Punctuation Review (34-40)	92

CONVENTIONS OF FORM AND APPEARANCE

82	Spelling: Typical problems I (41a)	94
83	Spelling: Typical problems II (41a)	95
84	Spelling: Rules (41b)	96
85	Hyphen (42)	97
86	Capital Letters I (43)	98
87	Capital Letters II (43)	99
88	Underlining or Italics I (44)	100
89	Underlining or Italics II (44)	101
90	Abbreviations I (45)	102
91	Abbreviations II (45)	103
92	Numbers I (46)	104
93	Numbers II (46)	105
94	Numbers III (46)	106
95	Avoiding Plagiarism and Documenting Sources I (50)	107
96	Avoiding Plagiarism and Documenting Sources II (50)	109
97	Avoiding Plagiarism and Documenting Sources: MLA (50, 52)	111
98	Avoiding Plagiarism and Documenting Sources: APA (50, 53)	113

CRITICAL THINKING

99	Critically Viewing Images (7b)	115

To the Student

This book emerged from the idea that you are a developing writer—not a beginning writer, not a remediating writer, certainly not an incompetent writer—but someone who, like all of us, is developing as a writer. And writing as it is developing, as you probably know, always has some areas that still need work. This exercise book is designed to provide help in those areas.

These exercises are built on the idea that good writing derives from correct, not flawed, writing. So for the most part you will be working with correct writing and finding ways to manipulate it. You will be invited to do some sentence combining and some sentence patterning, to transform sentences and paragraphs, to make substitutions and choices about preferred phrasings, to fill in some blanks, to identify parts of sentences, and, yes, in a few cases, to identify and correct errors. You will be able to write directly on these pages. Most of the exercises are written in connected discourse on topics of cross-disciplinary interest.

Because this book is coordinated with *The Little, Brown Compact Handbook*, 5th edition, by Jane Aaron, you are urged to study the related sections before doing each exercise. Those sections are identified at the top of each exercise; for example:

1. EMPHASIS: Beginnings and endings (11b)

This is the heading for the first exercise, its subject being emphasis as explained in section 11b of the *Handbook*. Each exercise is accompanied by an example to show how you can carry out the exercise.

1   EMPHASIS: Beginnings and Endings (11b)

To emphasize the importance of main ideas and to clarify meaning, combine each group of short sentences into a single sentence. Put the main ideas in main clauses, with the most important words near the beginning or ending of the sentences.

Example: The new hepatitis B vaccine is now available for infants.
   The new vaccine is also advised for teenagers.
   The new hepatitis B vaccine that is now available for infants is also advised for teenagers.

1. College students may not think about immunizations.
   They could be at risk.
   They could catch infectious diseases.

2. They are at greatest risk of contracting measles.
   They can catch it in crowded residence halls.

3. Some students have not had a measles booster.
   They could contract the disease when they go to college.

4. The shot you had as a baby may not be effective.
   You may need a booster now as an adult.

5. College students may need other booster shots.
   The shots would protect them from serious diseases.

6. People who are sexually active can catch hepatitis B.
   These people should get the hepatitis B series of shots.

7. People forget about tetanus boosters.
   Tetanus is a deadly illness.
   Everyone should have a booster every five to ten years.

8. Lyme disease is a debilitating illness.
   It is most often caused by infected ticks.
   It can be prevented with a new vaccination.

2 EMPHASIS: Coordinating Equal Ideas (11c)

Using coordination to emphasize equal ideas, combine each group of short sentences into a single sentence. Omit words and phrases that are unnecessarily repeated. (Related LBCH section: 12 Parallelism and 35 Commas.)

Example: Direct marketing raises issues about privacy.
Direct marketing raises issues about individual rights.
Direct marketing raises issues about privacy and individual rights.

1. Direct marketing uses databases to target consumers.
   It uses databases to target voters.
   It uses databases to target other groups.

2. Database information may include names.
   It may include addresses.
   It may include telephone numbers.
   It may include ages.
   It may include incomes.
   It may include other information.

3. The information may come from buyers' answers on warranty cards.
   It may also come from lists sold by banks.
   It may come from lists sold by credit card companies.

4. Sweepstakes contests are another source of database information.
   Motor vehicle departments are another source of database information.

5. The database can identify specific groups.
   And the database can personally address specific individuals.

6. Consumers often find direct marketing to be a nuisance.
   Voters feel the same way.

7. People can have their names removed from mailing lists.
   People can ask that their names not be sold.
   But the people have to take the initiative.

8. Databases are a powerful marketing tool.
   Databases are likely to continue to be used in direct marketing.

3   EMPHASIS: Subordinating Ideas (11d)

The following passage lacks emphasis because subordination does not distinguish main ideas from less important information. Decide which ideas are most important (and should be stated in main clauses) and which should be subordinated. Then revise the passage, changing words, phrases, or clauses as appropriate.

Example: Dresden is a city in eastern Germany and is the capital of Saxony. It is situated on the Elbe River and has a population of 481,000.
Dresden, a city in eastern Germany and the capital of Saxony, is situated on the Elbe River. It has a population of 481,000.

The city of Dresden, Germany, has had many troubles, but it remains an important city, and it plays an essential role in Germany's cultural tradition. In 1945 it was destroyed by Allied bombers and this is sometimes called the "Dresden Fire-Storm," and in it 135,000 people were killed, and many of the city's architectural landmarks were damaged. This wasn't the first time the city was destroyed by fire, for in 1491 it happened the first time, and in 1685 it happened again. Each time, the city has been rebuilt.

The city has also been the site of wartime occupation. It was occupied by Prussia during the War of the Austrian Succession, and that occupation ended in 1745 with the Treaty of Dresden, but the city was occupied again by Napoleon, and it was there that he won his last great victory, and that was called the Battle of Dresden. And of course the city was occupied by the Nazis during World War II, and this was the reason for the Dresden Fire-Storm.

There was not much standing in Dresden after the Fire-Storm, and this was unfortunate because Dresden had been noted for its architectural landmarks and for its rich collection of Italian, Dutch, and Flemish paintings, and its best-known product was Dresden china. But extensive rebuilding has been taking place since 1945, and the city is once again being called the German Florence.

4   EMPHASIS: Effective Subordination (11d)

Combine each pair of sentences, using the pronoun or connecting word in parentheses, so that less important information is subordinated to the main idea of the sentence.

Example: The dinosaurs roamed the earth. *(when)*
The landscape presented a very different appearance.
When the dinosaurs roamed the earth, the landscape presented a very different appearance.

1. The term *Jurassic* calls up images of battling dinosaurs.
   The dinosaurs are anachronisms on a lush present-day island. *(that)*

2. Dinosaurs were in fact a major life form. *(although)*
   The word *Jurassic* refers to the type of rock strata characteristic of the period.

3. The Jurassic Period occurred about 190 to 135 million years ago. *(which)*
   It had climates that were probably warm and moist.

4. The climate was mild. *(because)*
   Dinosaurs and other cold-blooded animals were able to thrive.

5. You are one of the millions who have seen the movie *Jurassic Park*. *(if)*
   You are no doubt familiar with *Tyrannosaurus* and *Brontosaurus*.

6. They were among the largest of the dinosaurs. *(because)*
   They seem to receive the most notice.

7. The dinosaurs are the most famous reptiles of the period. *(although)*
   Turtles and crocodiles also thrived at that time.

8. Flying reptiles such as the pterodactyls were common too.
   Birds also appeared during this time. *(although)*

9. We say that things of the past have "gone the way of the dinosaurs." *(though)*
   We still have remnants of the Jurassic Period with us today.

10. One of those survivors, the ginkgo tree, is valued today.
    It has exceptional tolerance for smog and drought. *(because)*

5 PARALLELISM: With *and, but, or, nor, yet* (12a)

Complete each sentence by underlining the most parallel and concise phrase.

Example:
The United States needs its National Guard to augment the active-duty army
- a. <u>and to serve as a local militia.</u>
- b. and serving as a local militia.
- c. and another service being to act as a local militia.

1. The US National Guard is a volunteer militia made up of army units
   - a. and air units.
   - b. and units connected with the Air Force.
   - c. and there are air units.

2. The units are located in the states and deal with civil disturbances
   - a. or natural disasters.
   - b. and with natural disasters.
   - c. and they help with natural disasters.

3. The Guard may be mobilized by the governors of the states
   - a. or the President of the United States may be mobilize it.
   - b. or by the President of the United States.
   - c. or it may be mobilized by the US President.

4. The National Guard was established in 1903 to be independent of the regular army
   - a. and at first it could be called up only by the state governors.
   - b. being subject to call-up by the state governors.
   - c. and to be subject to call-up by the state governors.

5. But a 1916 act of Congress made it subject to the President
   - a. and it was designated part of the US Army.
   - b. and part of the US Army.
   - c. and to be part of the US Army.

6. Under that act, the US Army had three components: the regular army, the reserves,
   - a. and the National Guard.
   - b. and the third was the National Guard.
   - c. the third being the National Guard.

7. During the Persian Gulf War of 1991, the regular army was supported by the reserves
   - a. and the National Guard.
   - b. and it was also supported by the National Guard.
   - c. duties also being performed by the National Guard.

6 PARALLELISM: with *both...and, either...or*, etc.; with lists and outlines (12a,b)

The following sentences require *both . . . and* or *either . . . or*. The _ mark indicates possible insertion points for the words in parentheses. Decide which is the appropriate location, and write the word above the mark.

Example: Companies can construct internship programs _ to meet _**both** short-term and long-term employment needs. (*both*)

1. Internships are win-win situations _ for _ students and employers. (*both*)

2. The student _ gains _ useful experience and makes valuable contacts. (*both*)

3. Internships are an asset for employers _ because the young workers are _ inexpensive and hardworking. (*both*)

4. The interns might be students _ in _ college or high school (*either*)

5. Oddly, the competition for internships is encountered _ by _ intern and by employer. (*both*)

6. Students line up for internship interviews _ with _ small businesses and with large corporations. (*both*)

7. Large corporations actively recruit college students who can bring to the company _ their eagerness _ to learn and their willingness to work. (*both*)

8. Many small businesses also seek out interns _ because _ they want _ the assistance from having qualified college students work for them or they would like the visibility with campus faculty and administrators. (*either*)

9. In some cases, students need to decide on an internship _ in _ this country or in Europe, Asia, or other foreign countries. (*either*)

10. After a successful internship, a college student might _ gain _ full-time employment at the internship company or take a job with a related company. (*either*)

7 VARIETY AND DETAILS (13)

Improve the interest and texture of the following passage by adding details at each _ mark that reflect the attitude of the author. Change the articles *a* or *an* if necessary.

                                                                  knotty   softhearted

Example: Feral, or undomesticated, cats can be a _ problem for the _ householder.

Last winter a _ feral cat adopted my back yard. With a _ householder to set out _ food and water, she was all set. It might have been a _ and comfortable life if not for the _ _ of a Minnesota winter. But somehow, with a _ fur coat and the _ protection of a fallen _ tree, she made it through the _ cold.

But by early spring it was apparent that she was pregnant. One day she came back into the yard looking much leaner and _ , and from then on I could _ see her stalking chipmunks. She was a _ hunter; I could tell by the number of _ chipmunks she carried off to her family. In fact, she nearly cleaned the yard of the little _ critters. Of course, I continued feeding her from the _ bags of _ cat food I bought from Pet Food Warehouse.

I kept wondering when she was going to bring her _ offspring to the food source. Last week it happened: _ little _ furballs bouncing around in the yard, apparently oblivious to the fact that _ people lived in the house and that this _ playground was not a _ extension of their _ nest in the woods. But they soon found out–when the food dish was empty and I went out to refill it. Now _ little _ furballs scattered every which way–under the gazebo, into the woods, under the tree. But not their mother. She knew where the food came from, and even though she was _ wary and would not let me come close enough to touch her, she was reluctant to go too far away.

So now I have a _ problem : _ _ kittens emptying a food bowl in minutes, growing bigger every day, becoming feral cats just like their mother. And someday, unless I take some _ action first, they will add to the feral population. Something must be done, but they're all so _ !

8 APPROPRIATE AND EXACT LANGUAGE: Appropriate language (14a)

In this memo written to the author's supervisor, some of the language is inappropriate for the situation. Make corrections so that it is written in the type of direct English expected in business.

Example: ~~Persuant to~~ **Regarding** the next sales meeting, I'll ~~let the cat out of the bag~~ **inform** you when we're ready.

January 23, 2000

To: Jane Bascomb
From: Robert Campbell
Subject: Report on Carbondale Trip

As per your request for a written report on my sales trip to Carbondale, I am herewith stating the events that occurred. In a word, the trip was a bummer. As we arranged, I departed on January 17 via Magellanic Airlines. After waiting for deicing and for snowplowing the runway and then a delayed landing, I was going crazy by the time I finally disembarked from the plane and took off for the meeting. I arrived just in time to see everyone else heading for the exit.

However, I did manage to salvage part of the day. I grabbed Joe Cosner as he was leaving and spent a couple of hours with him figuring out how we might put Ajax's nose out of joint by transcending their service record. This one-upmanship may cost us a pretty penny, but, in my opinion, it's worth whatever it costs.

Well, that was the high point of the trip. The next day, none of my appointments showed, so I ended up twiddling my thumbs in my hotel room until time to catch the flight back. You'll find attached herewith all the receipts for my meals and taxi. As usual, airfare and lodging are covered on the company plastic.

9   APPROPRIATE AND EXACT LANGUAGE: Biased language (14a)

Revise the following sentences to eliminate biased language. If you convert singular usage to plural, be sure to make any other changes that might be required.

Example: ~~The career placement officer~~ **Career placement officers** at most colleges and universities will spend part of ~~his~~ **their** time advising students on how to write successful résumés.

1. When a person applies for a job, he should represent himself with the best possible résumé.

2. A person applying for a job as mailman should appear to be honest and responsible.

3. Someone applying for a position as an in-home nurse should also represent herself as honest and responsible.

4. Of course, she should also have a background of capable nursing.

5. The businessman who is scanning a stack of résumés will, of necessity, read them all quickly.

6. So the person who wants his résumé to stand out will make sure it highlights his best points.

7. The computer programmer will highlight his experience with computers.

8. Volunteer work may be appropriate too, for example being chairman of a student organization.

9. If the student has been secretary for a campus organization, she could include that volunteer experience on her résumé.

10. If everyone writing a résumé would keep in mind the guy who will be reading it, the applicant might know better what he should include and how he should format that information.

10 APPROPRIATE AND EXACT LANGUAGE: Exact Language (14b)

Underline the word(s) that best convey the meaning of each sentence. If you need help, refer to your dictionary or to the glossary at the back of your handbook.

Example: Some people get [*nauseated, nauseous*] just thinking about how much money other people have.

1. Don't you wish you had the problem of finding [*someplace, somewhere*] to invest a few hundred thousand dollars?

2. Some people who have that much money like to [*flaunt, flout*] it.

3. Others are totally [*disinterested, uninterested*] in whether others know how much money they have.

4. Their [*idea, ideal*] of wealth is to accept their good fortune and not let their [*conscience, conscious*] bother them about other people.

5. They [*precede, proceed*] with their lives with no worries about paying the rent or buying the groceries.

6. And they give little thought to what their lives would be like if they were to [*lose, loose*] their money.

7. There are other people, however, who are [*literally, nearly*] starving for lack of sufficient money to buy groceries.

8. Their lives are very [*different from, different than*] the lives of the wealthy.

9. They [*wait on, wait for*] a better day when they can [*leave, let*] their worries go.

10. Being a college student is like that, because the [*unique, most unique*] feature of student life is never having enough money.

11. But even though poverty is [*implicit, explicit*] in a college education, the student can [*imply, infer*] that there is a potential job following the degree.

11 APPROPRIATE AND EXACT LANGUAGE: Idioms (14b)

Complete the following sentences by filling the blanks with the appropriate prepositions from this list: *at, by, for, from, in, of, on, to, with.*

Example: The most recent amendment _to_ the US Constitution was proposed _by_ Congress _in_ 1789 and ratified _in_ 1992.

1. The Eighteenth Amendment _____ the Constitution _____ the United States was ratified _____ 1919.
2. It prohibited the "manufacture, sale, or transportation _____ intoxicating liquors."
3. It was adopted _____ response _____ a nationwide crusade _____ temperance groups.
4. One _____ those groups was the Women's Christian Temperance Union.
5. The amendment was defined _____ Congress _____ the Volstead Act.
6. The Act was vetoed _____ President Woodrow Wilson, but Congress passed it over his veto.
7. The Amendment did not prevent Americans _____ drinking, and the sale _____ alcoholic beverages was taken over _____ organized crime.
8. _____ the demand _____ liquor came wide-scale smuggling and bootlegging.
9. _____ 1919 _____ 1933, when the Amendment was repealed, gangs such as that led _____ Al Capone _____ Chicago controlled the sale _____ alcohol.
10. The Twenty-First Amendment, passed _____ 1933, is the only amendment passed _____ the purpose _____ repealing an earlier amendment.
11. Other laws regarding the sale _____ intoxicating liquors remained _____ effect.
12. We still have laws _____ the regulation _____ licenses and _____ taxes related _____ the liquor industry.

12 APPROPRIATE AND EXACT LANGUAGE: Confusing language (14 and 41a)

From the options given in brackets, underline the form that is correct in the context of each sentence.

Example: [Setting, <u>Sitting</u>] in a small city called Pisa, only a short drive from Florence, Italy, is one of the most famous buildings in the world, the Leaning Tower.

The top of the tower, [raising, rising] 177 feet above the ground, is approximately 16 feet out of line with [its, it's] base. The tower served as the bell tower of a cathedral [laying, lying] only a short distance away and was constructed between 1173 and 1372 by Roman Catholic priests. After the first three stories were completed, the priests realized that the building was tipping [to, too, two] the side, but no one could [fine, fined, find] the reason for the shift. The priests debated [weather, whether] they should move the tower to a [knew, new] location, but that would [have, of] delayed the project for almost a century. Therefore, on the [advice, advise] of architects, the priests decided to continue building the tower at the original [cite, sight, site]. In [an, and] attempt to correct the problem, they changed the angle of the remaining floors so that the top of the tower was actually straighter [than, then] the middle. The angle that the tower leans has increased as time has [passed, past]. This imbalance greatly [affects, effects] how someone climbs the spiraling steps to the top. On the side that leans toward the ground, walking up the steps is easy. However, on the side that leans away, the gravitational pull makes walking much more difficult. Frequently, people [loose, lose] [their, there, they're] [breath, breathe] and must pause midway to the top.

13   CONCISENESS: Focusing on subject and verb, cutting empty words and repetition, reducing clauses and phrases (16a,b,c,d)

Read the following paragraphs, focusing on the subject and verb in each sentence. Cross out all needless repetition and empty words and phrases, and make the paragraphs less wordy by reducing modifiers. You may need to revise other parts of the sentences as well. Do not cut words that contribute meaning.

Example: ~~At the present time, the incidence of bankruptcies is~~ **Bankruptcies are** increasing ~~in numbers~~.

The use of credit cards may be the major and most important reason why people file for bankruptcy. In the situation of personal bankruptcy, people say that the easy and effortless availability of credit cards has, in a manner of speaking, pushed them over the edge and required that they declare themselves insolvent and totally without financial resources. Many of these people claim to have been in possession of ten or more credit cards, and another large and greatly significant proportion say they have six to nine cards.

Due to the fact that credit cards are readily issued to young adults, the age group of eighteen- to twenty-nine-year-olds is filing for personal bankruptcy in large numbers. Their easy access to credit cards contributes to the second cause of financial failure for the twenty-somethings: mismanagement of their finances. For all intents and purposes, they live beyond their means. As the charges add up and increase in size, the card companies graciously extend the lines of credit. Then one day the card holders realize they are in over their heads and can't possibly pay off the ever-increasing size of their debt. "I never asked for the credit cards," they say. But by virtue of the fact that they used them, they are responsible for paying the bills.

In addition to the stigma that goes along with bankruptcy, there are other undesirable and unwanted consequences of filing for bankruptcy. One is that the bankruptcy remains on people's credit record for six to ten years depending on the type of filing they did. Also, they may be unable to rent an apartment or get a mortgage, and if they do manage to get a loan they may have to pay additional fees or a higher interest rate. Last but not least, they will still have to pay some kinds of bills, such as student loans, child support, and taxes.

14 CONCISENESS: Using strong verbs and active voice, cutting *there is*, combining sentences, rewriting jargon (16a,e,f,g)

Edit the following sentences to strengthen verbs, change passive voice to active, eliminate forms of *there is* and *it is* at the beginnings of clauses, and eliminate jargon. Combing sentences when doing so reduces wordiness.

Example: It is thought by some people that when it comes to exercise there is no gain without pain.
Some people think that pain is a necessary part of exercise.

1. If sore muscles after exercising are a problem for you, there are some things that can be done to ease the discomfort.

2. First, the immediate application of cold can reduce inflammation.

3. Blood vessels are constricted by cold. Blood is kept away from the injured muscles.

4. The avoidance of heat for the first day is advisable.

5. The application of heat within the first twenty-four hours can cause an increase in muscle soreness and stiffness.

6. There are two ways the application of cold can be made: with a cold shower or an ice pack.

7. Inflammation of muscles can also be reduced with medication that is anti-inflammatory, such as aspirin and ibuprofen.

8. You can forget so-called sports creams, because the real problem lies much deeper.

9. While the healing is taking place, you need to take it easy.

10. A day or two after overdoing the exercise, it is advisable for you to get some light exercise and gentle massage.

11. Overdoing the exercise is not a requirement for physical fitness.

15 PARTS OF SPEECH: Nouns, pronouns, verbs (17a,b,c)

Identify the words that function as nouns, pronouns, and verbs in these sentences by noting *N, P,* or *V* in the space above them.

Example: The ginkgo tree has a second name: it is also called the maidenhair tree.
(N V   N P V   V   N)

A relic from the age of the dinosaurs, the ginkgo tree is descended from the family Ginkgoaceae, which lived 175 to 200 million years ago. The tree grows to about 120 feet in height and has fan-shaped leaves that are about three inches wide. As a deciduous tree, it loses its leaves in the fall after they turn a bright yellow.

The ginkgo is a member of the tree family called gymnosperms. Trees in this family do not get flowers. Instead, they produce seeds similar to the cones of evergreen trees. The fruit of the ginkgo looks something like a plum. It grows about one inch long and is orange-yellow when ripe. It has a large white seed that is valued as a food in parts of Asia.

The tree is esteemed in the United States and Europe as an ornamental shade tree. It is often used to line streets and parkways. One of its features is its great tolerance for smoke, low temperatures, and low rainfall, making it ideal for many cities. A shortcoming, however, is the foul odor of its fruit. Because only the female tree bears fruit, the male is preferred for ornamental purposes.

The ginkgo is not native to North America. It was introduced from southeastern China, where it is native and where it is cultivated for its seeds. The Chinese also use ginkgo extracts as a medicine.

The ginkgo we know is the only remaining species of the many types of ginkgo that were common during the Jurassic Period, when they developed. A visit to a real Jurassic Park would reveal ginkgos as common as the oak and maple are today.

16   PARTS OF SPEECH: Nouns and verbs (17a,c)

In each of the following sentences, the same word is used as both a noun and a verb. Identify the function by writing *N* or *V* above the underlined words.

                                                       V   N

Example: The electrician <u>wired</u> the house with heavy-duty <u>wire</u>.

1. Because of her broken leg, the president <u>chaired</u> the meeting from her <u>chair</u>.

2. The envelope had been <u>stapled</u> so securely that we couldn't remove the last <u>staple</u>.

3. We will <u>house</u> as many visitors as we can in the fraternity <u>house</u>.

4. If you <u>train</u> your binoculars closely, you can see that distant <u>train</u>.

5. We'll <u>tape</u> the concert if we can find another <u>tape</u>.

6. You can <u>telephone</u> me from the public <u>telephone</u> in the station.

7. If the <u>fax</u> hadn't been broken, we'd have <u>faxed</u> you the figures.

8. The last page of the <u>book</u> explained how a person could <u>book</u> cruises.

9. Despite the intense <u>heat</u>, the elderly man was still <u>heating</u> the room.

10. The <u>subjects</u> of the research were <u>subjected</u> to all kinds of tests.

11. I'll <u>water</u> my plants with the <u>water</u> from the dehumidifier.

12. When you find your <u>hammer</u>, will you <u>hammer</u> these boards together?

13. Because the batteries in the <u>radio</u> were dead, the captain could not <u>radio</u> for help.

14. The mayor <u>tabled</u> the motion with a loud bang of his gavel on the <u>table</u>.

15. The beagle treed the cat and then stood barking at the foot of the tree.

16. As the contractor papered the wall, I suddenly realized that I hated the paper.

17. If you box those materials properly, the box won't come undone.

18. We dated the letter when it arrived, but we realize now that our date was wrong.

17   PARTS OF SPEECH: Adjectives and adverbs (17d)

Change the following sentences by replacing each underlined word with another word. Then tell whether you substituted an adjective (*adj*) or an adverb (*adv*).

Example: Some people are stressed when they don't actually need to be.
                    Many (adj)   **even** (adv)

1. You can reduce your stress level by adopting a few easy changes in your life.

2. One is to get up fifteen minutes earlier than you ordinarily need to.

3. Another is to eat a good breakfast, and eat it slowly enough to enjoy it.

4. To keep from being stressed about everything you have to do, make a list of those things and cross them off as you complete them.

5. Do your unpleasant tasks early in the day.

6. Get enough rest and some brisk exercise.

7. Be good; do good; laugh more.

8. Every day, do at least one thing you really enjoy.

9. If waiting in lines is stressful for you, carry reading material when you know you'll have to wait.

10. Don't worry about those things you don't have any control over.

11. Listen more; talk less.

12. Eat well, but eat less food.

13. Make promises sparingly and keep them faithfully.

14. Plan ahead to prevent some worries.

15. For example, carry an extra car key, and you won't be locked out of your car.

16. See your doctor and dentist regularly, and keep your car well maintained.

18   PARTS OF SPEECH: Connecting words (17e)

Fill in the blank spaces with the appropriate connecting words: a preposition for a single underline, a subordinating conjunction for a double underline, and a coordinating conjunction for a dotted line. (Consult the lists in the handbook if you need help selecting these words.)

Example: A Trojan priest warned, "Beware __of__ Greeks bearing gifts."

1. Just about everyone has heard the story _____ the Trojan Horse.

2. It describes an incident _____ occurred _____ the end _____ the Trojan War.

3. It happened _____ the city _____ Troy .... was planned _____ the Greeks.

4. The Greeks built a huge wooden horse _____ was hollow inside .... big enough to hold many men.

5. _____ night, they rolled the horse _____ the gate _____ Troy .... left it there.

6. Then they moved their ships out _____ sight _____ Troy.

7. _____ the morning, the Trojans were astonished to see the enormous horse.

8. .... they were more surprised to see _____ the Greeks had departed.

9. _____ they were curious to examine this gift _____ the Greeks, they dragged the horse _____ the city .... left it outside the temple _____ they rejoiced _____ the end _____ the war.

10. _____ the middle _____ the night, the Greeks emerged _____ the horse .... began setting fires all _____ town.

11. _____ the Trojan soldiers awoke .... came out _____ their houses, the Greeks killed them one _____ one.

12. The Trojans put up a noble fight, ... the Greeks had the upper hand.

13. _____ the next morning, the Trojan men were dead .... the women were slaves _____ the Greeks.

19   THE SENTENCE: Subject and predicate (18a)

In each sentence, draw a vertical line between the subject and the predicate. Then underline each simple subject once and each verb twice.

Example: The <u>pony</u>, the light <u>horse</u>, and the draft <u>horse</u>   /   <u>are</u> the three main types of horses.

1. The <u>horse</u> / <u>has</u> a long history of serving humanity but today <u>is</u> mainly a show and sport animal.

2. A member of the genus *Equus*, the domestic <u>horse</u> / <u>is related</u> to the wild Przewalski's horse, the ass, and the zebra.

3. The domestic <u>horse</u> and its <u>relatives</u> / <u>are</u> all herbivorous plains-dwelling herd animals.

4. An average-sized adult <u>horse</u> / <u>may require</u> 26 pounds or more of pasture feed or hay per day.

5. Racing <u>horses</u> / <u>require</u> some grain for part of their forage.

6. Oddly, the modern <u>horse</u> / <u>evolved</u> in North America and then <u>became</u> extinct here after spreading to other parts of the world.

7. <u>It</u> / <u>was reintroduced</u> here by the Spaniards, profoundly affecting the culture of Native Americans.

8. The North American <u>animals</u> called wild horses / <u>are</u> actually <u>descended</u> from escaped domesticated horses.

9. There / <u>are</u> <u>records</u> of horses having been hunted and domesticated as early as four to five thousand years ago.

10. The earliest <u>ancestor</u> of the modern horse / <u>may have been</u> eohippus, approximately 55 million years ago.

20   THE SENTENCE: Predicate patterns (18b)

Each of these numbered sentences represents one predicate pattern. Using the short sentences below each pattern, construct a sentence that follows the same pattern. Then identify your subject (*S*) and verb (*V*), plus any direct objects (*DO*), indirect objects (*IO*), subject complements (*SC*), or object complements (*OC*).

Example:
Overall crime did not decrease in the West. (*subject, verb*)
　　Serious crime did decrease.
　　It decreased in the Northeast.
　　　　　S　　　V　　V
　　Serious crime did decrease in the Northeast.

1. The number of serious crimes in the United States decreased in the early 1990s. (*subject, verb*)
　　Serious crimes declined.
　　They were most kinds of serious crimes.
　　The decline occurred in each year.

2. The Crime Index measures serious crime. (*subject, verb, direct object*)
　　The Federal Bureau of Investigation invented something.
　　It invented the Crime Index.

3. The four serious violent crimes are murder, robbery, forcible rape, and aggravated assault. (*subject, verb, four subject complements*)
　　There are four serious property crimes.
　　The first is motor vehicle theft.
　　Another is burglary.
　　Another serious property crime is arson.
　　The last is larceny-theft.

4. The Crime Index gives the FBI a measure of crime. (*subject, verb, indirect object, direct object*)
   Some cities are the largest.
   Those cities showed the FBI something.
   They had the largest decline in crime.

5. The Crime Index makes trends apparent in its reports. (*subject, verb, direct object, object complement*)
   Some cities are smaller.
   Those cities prove something.
   The decline is unrepresentative of the nation.

21   PHRASES AND SUBORDINATE CLAUSES: Phrases (19a)

Rewrite the following sentences, replacing each underlined clause with a phrase that begins with the word(s) in parentheses. Then tell what kind of phrase you used.

Example: Modern English contains words <u>that were borrowed from many sources</u>. (*borrowed*)
Modern English contains words borrowed from many sources. (participle)

1. <u>Because it has many words with similar meanings,</u> English can make choosing the appropriate word difficult. (*Because of*)

2. <u>Because it has borrowed words from other languages such as French and Latin,</u> English has many words with similar meanings. (*having borrowed*)

3. <u>When one has so many words to choose from,</u> how does a writer decide between *motherly* and *maternal*, for example, or between *womanly, feminine,* or *female*? (*Having*)

4. Some people have recommended the longer and more ornate words, <u>which would avoid the flatness of shortened words.</u> (*to avoid*)

5. During the Renaissance there was a heated debate between the Latinists, <u>who favored words derived from Latin</u>, and the Saxonists, <u>who preferred the native Anglo-Saxon words</u>. (*favoring; preferring*)

6. Students in writing classes are often told that they should choose the shorter word. (*to choose*)

7. The implication is that they should seek out the Anglo-Saxon, or Old English, word. (*to seek*)

8. Better advice, according to William Hazlitt, is the principle that a person should choose "the best word in common use." (*of choosing*)

9. If one were to keep this principle in mind, a person would choose *womanly*, which is the Anglo-Saxon word, or *feminine*, which is a French derivative, according to meaning and situation. (*To keep, the Anglo-Saxon, a French*)

10. Synonyms rarely have the same meaning, because usage has defined differences. (*usage having*)

11. The Old English word *handbook*, for example, doesn't have quite the same meaning as the French derivative *manual*, which is a synonym. (*a synonym*)

12. English may seem to be a largely borrowed language, but its most frequently repeated words–which are the pronouns, articles, conjunctions, and prepositions–are largely Old English in derivation. (*the pronouns*)

22   PHRASES AND SUBORDINATE CLAUSES: Clauses (19b)

Identify the type of each underlined subordinate clause: adjective (*adj*), adverb (*adv*), or noun (*n*). For each noun clause, tell its function in the sentence: subject (*S*), direct object (*DO*), object of preposition (*OP*), or subject complement (*SC*).

Example:

__adv__   Because the Koran is written in Arabic, Muslims refer to God as Allah, the Arabic word for his name.

_____ 1. The Prophet Muhammad, who was born about AD 570 in the city of Mecca, is the founder of Islam.

_____ 2. He grew up in the care of his grandfather and an uncle, because both of his parents had died.

_____ 3. His family was part of a powerful Arab tribe that lived in western Arabia.

_____ 4. When he was about 40 years old, he had a vision in a cave outside Mecca.

_____ 5. In the vision, God called him to preach to the people and warn them that the day of judgment was coming.

_____ 6. Throughout his life, he continued to have revelations, which have been written in the Koran.

_____ 7. The Koran is the sacred book of the Muslims, who as adherents of Islam view Muhammad as God's messenger.

_____ 8. When he no longer had the support of the clans of Mecca, he and his followers moved to Medina.

_____ 9. There they established an organized Muslim community that soon had armed clashes with Meccans and Jewish clans.

_____ 10. Despite hostilities between the two cities, the Muslims of Medina regarded Mecca as the holy city and began facing that direction when they worshiped.

_____ 11. Muhammad continued as the religious, political, and military leader of Islam, which spread in Asia and Africa.

_____ 12. He died in 632, but the legacy of Islam lived on as it became one of the three great monotheistic religions.

23 SENTENCE TYPES (20)

Identify the following sentences as simple (a single main clause), compound (two or more main clauses), complex (a main clause and at least one subordinate clause), or compound-complex (*CC*, two or more main clauses and at least one subordinate clause).

Example:

complex   The human voice is produced in the larynx, a section of the throat that has two bands called vocal chords.

_____ 1. Our world has many sounds, but all the sounds have one thing in common.

_____ 2. The one thing that all sounds share is that they are produced by vibrations.

_____ 3. The vibrations make the air move in waves, and these sound waves travel to the ear.

_____ 4. When sound waves enter the ear, the brain has to interpret them.

_____ 5. Sound waves can also travel through other material, such as water and even the solid earth.

_____ 6. Some sounds are pleasant, and others, which we call noise, are not.

_____ 7. Most noises are produced by irregular vibrations at irregular intervals; an example is the barking of a dog.

_____ 8. Some noises are called *impulsive sounds*, because they start suddenly and die quickly.

_____ 9. A gunshot is an example of an impulsive sound; the noise of a power lawnmower is a series of impulsive sounds.

_____ 10. Sounds have frequency and pitch.

_____ 11. The more rapidly an object vibrates, the higher the frequency and the pitch.

_____ 12. Musical instruments can produce a wide range of pitches.

_____ 13. People can hear a wide range of sounds, but dogs and cats can hear sounds with higher frequencies.

_____ 14. However, dogs have a narrow range of sounds they can produce, and cats have an even narrower range.

24 VERB FORMS: Irregular verbs (21a,b)

For each sentence below, underline the correct form of the irregular verb from the choices given in brackets.

> *Example:* The books were [*hid*, *hidden*] under some old magazines that had been [*laid*, *layed*, *lain*] on top of them.

1. Patrick has [*went, gone*] to the library and has [*took, taken, taked*] back some overdue books.

2. He [*letted, let*] the librarian know that he would have [*bringed, brought*] the books back sooner if he could have [*drove, driven, drived*] his car.

3. But somebody had [*stole, stolen, stealed*] his car, which he had just [*buyed, bought*] used at Bob's Used Car Lot.

4. The police had finally [*caught, catched*] the car thief and had [*spoke, spoken, speaked*] to Patrick's wife about where he could pick up the car.

5. The directions they had [*gave, gived, given*] her were confusing and [*lead, led, leaded*] to a dead-end road.

6. He and the friend who was driving him finally [*chose, chosen, choosed, choose*] the right direction after having [*come, came, coming*] on the wrong one twice.

7. Arriving at the impound lot, they [*finded, found, founded*] his car [*sitting, setting*] by itself in a corner and looking beat up.

8. It looked as if someone had [*threw, thrown, throwed*] rocks at it and had [*wore, worn, weared*] the paint off in several places, though at least it seemed to be in one piece.

9. Then he saw that a tire had been [*blew, blown, blowed*] and some kind of acid must have [*ate, eaten, eat*] away some paint on the trunk.

10. He had started the engine and had [*ran, run, runned*] it for a while to find out how it sounded, but then he had [*seen, saw, seed*] that the gas tank was about empty.

11. So he [*cut, cutted*] the engine to conserve gas and [*got, gotten, getted*] out to look underneath.

12. He [*laid, lay, lied*] down under the car to look for damage there, but when he [*rose, raised, rised*] up he [*give, gave, gived*] his head a nasty bump.

13. The librarian thought this was quite a tale, better than any he had [*heared, heard*] in quite some time, so what he [*did, done*] was tell Patrick he could [*forget, forgot, forgotten*] the fine for the late books.

14. But Patrick [*drawed, draw, drew*] out his wallet and [*begin, began, begun*] to take out money, which he [*shown, shone, showed, show*] to the librarian.

15. "I [*knowed, known, know, knew*] I shouldn't have [*keep, kept, keeped*] those books so long," he said as he [*hold, held, holded*] out his hand.

16. "It would have been worse if you had [*lose, loose, lost, lossed*] them," [*say, said, sayed*] the librarian, who [*wrote, written*] a receipt for the $10 fine.

17. They [*shaked, shaken, shook*] hands after Patrick had [*paid, payed, pay*] the fine.

18. After Patrick [*leave, left*], the librarian [*lay, laid, lain*] the returned books on the shelf.

25   VERB FORMS: -s and -ed forms (21c)

Revise the underlined verbs in the following paragraphs so that they describe present events instead of past events.

Example: Reflective aluminum <u>coated</u> (coats) the CD disk, and transparent plastic <u>protected</u> (protects) it.

A compact disk (CD) player <u>reproduced</u> sound by using a laser beam to read a pattern of pits on a disk. Rather than sound vibrations like those recorded on plastic phonograph records or tapes, the CD <u>played</u> music by number. A series of 1s and 0s <u>represented</u> individual sounds. No matter how subtle, any variation in sound <u>translated</u> from the numbers to the sound emitted by the player. On the disk, the 1s and 0s <u>looked</u> like microscopic pits. A 1 <u>appeared</u> as a pit, a 0 as a space within or between pits. A single disk <u>carried</u> as many as billions of pits.

The laser beam <u>interpreted</u> the 1s and 0s as tone, volume, pitch, and so on. To read the pits and spaces, the beam <u>entered</u> a prism that <u>reflected</u> the beam onto the underside of the disk. A pit <u>scattered</u> and <u>reflected</u> the laser beam weakly. But a smooth space <u>reflected</u> it strongly. The reflected light then <u>traveled</u> back through the prism, which <u>directed</u> it onto a photodetector. With other electronic devices, the detector <u>converted</u> the light to 1s and 0s again. Then circuits <u>converted</u> the 1s and 0s to electrical waves like those that a phonograph record <u>produced</u>. Amplifiers and speakers <u>produced</u> a sound that <u>surpassed</u> what came from the old systems.

The CD player reproduced sound much more accurately and with much less distortion. Because only light touched the disk, the new system eliminated the distortion caused by a needle moving through a groove. It also avoided the scratchy and clicking noises from imperfections and dust on the record. The distortion that sometimes occurred with tapes disappeared too with the CD system. In addition, the compact disk allowed a person to skip around to listen to selected parts of the disk.

26   VERB FORMS: Helping verbs (21d)

Fill in each blank with one of the helping verbs from the list below.

be	being	does	would
is	been	has	can
are	do	have	will

Example: Color television pictures __are__ created by the mixing of colored lights.

1. Colors _____ be produced in a tremendous variety.

2. They _____ mixed in one of two ways.

3. By mixing colorants, artists and designers _____ produced a great variety of colors.

4. Powdered chemical substances that produce color _____ known as colorants.

5. A colorant that dissolves in a liquid _____ called a dye.

6. Colorants that _____ not dissolve but remain as solid particles _____ called pigments.

7. If a person mixed two colorants, a third color _____ be produced.

8. Each color in the mixture would _____ absorbing some of the wavelengths of light.

9. Red, yellow, and blue have _____ designated the three primary colorants, or the primary colors in paint.

10. Mixing the three primary colorants in equal amounts _____ produce black.

11. There is a second way of mixing colors, and it definitely _____ differ from colorant mixing.

12. This method _____ been termed "mixing colored lights."

13. Color mixtures _____ produced when colored lights projected on a screen each contribute light wavelengths.

14. Red, yellow, and green are now _____ called the primary colors of light.

15. Mixing the three together in the proper proportions _____ produce white light.

27   VERB FORMS: Verb + gerund or infinitive (21e)

Finish each sentence by underlining the correct gerund or infinitive ending. In some cases, both endings are correct.

Example: Teachers will usually
a. <u>ask students to write academic papers.</u>
b. ask to write academic papers.
c. ask students writing academic papers.

1. Writers usually have an idea in mind
   a. when they begin to write.
   b. when they begin writing.
   c. (either one)

2. But sometimes they
   a. have to think awhile before beginning.
   b. have thinking awhile before beginning.
   c. (either one)

3. And sometimes they must
   a. force to begin.
   b. force themselves to begin.
   c. force beginning.

4. Ideas often come more easily once writers
   a. start writing.
   b. start to write.
   c. (either one)

5. The act of writing seems
   a. to let the ideas to come.
   b. to let the ideas come.
   c. to let the ideas coming.

6. Once they have begun, writers
   a. may actually enjoy writing.
   b. may actually enjoy to write.
   c. (either one)

7. They may even
   a. want to tell the reader about their ideas.
   b. want telling the reader about their ideas.
   c. want themselves to tell the reader about their ideas.

28 VERB FORMS: Verb + particle (21f)

In each group, underline the sentence that correctly combines verbs and particles. If both are correct, underline both sentences.

Example:

    a.   <u>When employers look résumés over, they often include volunteer work.</u>

    b.   <u>When employers look over résumés, they often include volunteer work.</u>

1. a. Many students look into doing volunteer work.
   b. Many students look volunteer work into doing.

2. a. They want to fill their experience out with volunteer work.
   b. They want to fill out their experience with volunteer work.

3. a. If they luckily come across volunteer work in their field, they take it.
   b. If they come luckily across volunteer work in their field, they take it.

4. a. Doing volunteer work may help them make their minds up about their careers.
   b. Doing volunteer work may help them make up their minds about their careers.

5. a. At the same time, they are helping other people out.
   b. At the same time, they are helping out other people.

6. a. While they are helping out them, the volunteers are also acquiring skills.
   b. While they are helping them out, the volunteers are also acquiring skills.

7. a. They may learn nursing skills by frequently taking care of elderly people.
   b. They may learn nursing skills by taking care frequently of elderly people.

8. a. But students aren't always able to run into career-oriented volunteer work.
   b. But students aren't always able to run career-oriented volunteer work into.

9. a. Sometimes they need to turn a volunteer job down.
   b. Sometimes they need to turn down a volunteer job.

10. a. They shouldn't call off the search after only one offer.
    2. They shouldn't call the search off after only one offer.

29   VERB TENSES: Present and perfect (22a,b)

Change each underlined verb to present or present perfect tense to make the paragraphs read as if events are happening now.

Example: Finding competent generals <u>had been</u> **has been** a trial for Abraham Lincoln.

One of the least known union generals of the American Civil War <u>was</u> William Rosecrans. But his name <u>was</u> a familiar one to President Lincoln. Rosecrans apparently <u>spent</u> as much time writing letters as he <u>did</u> commanding his troops. The letters <u>were</u> mostly angry and bickering, complaining that he <u>had</u> not been getting the support he <u>believed</u> he should have. And he always <u>seemed</u> to think that he <u>had</u> to explain in great detail why he <u>had</u> not acted in a particular way–for example, the way his commander-in-chief, the President, <u>had</u> expected him to act.

In one letter to Lincoln, he <u>tried</u> to show why he <u>had</u> not been in Vicksburg as Lincoln <u>had</u> expected him to be. He further <u>explained</u> how his long supply line and his lack of sufficient cavalry <u>made</u> it difficult for him to move any faster. He <u>was</u> sure the President <u>was</u> dissatisfied with his work. In a carefully phrased letter, Lincoln <u>replied</u> that he <u>was</u> not dissatisfied with Rosecrans and still <u>had</u> confidence in his ability to lead his troops. However, Lincoln staunchly <u>reiterated</u> his earlier order that Rosecrans should move to Vicksburg to lend reinforcement to General Grant. He <u>did</u> not agree with Rosecrans's reasoning and <u>stated</u> that Rosecrans's position <u>was</u> going to be more difficult now as a result of his failure to move. He <u>ended</u> by urging Rosecrans to quit worrying and to take action.

But Rosecrans sent Lincoln another argumentative letter, again bringing up his Vicksburg opinion. His intent seemed to be to prove the President wrong and himself right. He must have been quite a trial for Lincoln. A little more than two months later, Lincoln turned over to Grant the command of Rosecrans's army and told Grant he could retain Rosecrans or replace him. Grant chose to replace him, and Lincoln approved.

30 VERB TENSES: Progressive (22c)

Underline the correct form of each verb from the choices given in brackets.

Example: Many Americans and people elsewhere in the world [*are wanting,* <u>*want*</u>] to visit Yellowstone National Park.

1. Scientists [*are still studying, still study, are still studied*] the geologic forces at work in Yellowstone National Park.

2. They [*are understanding, understand, are understood*] some of the secrets below the surface.

3. They [*are knowing, know, are known*], for example, that earthquakes are the main cause of altered geyser schedules.

4. Some geysers [*are having, have*] regular schedules of shooting columns of water and steam into the air, and others [*are being, are*] very unpredictable.

5. Some geysers [*are no longer erupting, are no longer erupted*] because careless visitors have thrown trash into them, choking them off.

6. The geysers and the boiling hot springs [*are showing, show*] the immense heat that lurks below the surface.

7. Pools of mud or water [*are bubbling, are bubbled*] madly in the heat.

8. Visitors [*have been extolling, have extolled*] its marvels for years.

9. Their friends sometimes suspect that the visitors [*are exaggerating, are exaggerated*] about the splendid sights.

10. Can you imagine the trouble the first visitor had when he [*was trying, was tried*] to convince other people of what he had seen?

11. John Colter, that first visitor, [*was seeing, saw, was seen*] Yellowstone in 1807.

31   VERB TENSES: Consistency and sequence (22d,e)

Change any underlined verb whose tense either is inconsistent with the tenses of other verbs in the passage (but it does not reflect actual changes in time) or is not in correct sequence (because the tense in the subordinate clause is not appropriate for the tense in the main clause). Many of the verbs are correct.

Example: Lowly mortals <u>were</u> wise to stay out of the way when a Roman god
became
<u>becomes</u> angry.

The ancient Romans <u>had</u> a story that <u>explained</u> the skill of spiders in weaving their complex webs. In the story, the goddess Minerva, who <u>was</u> known as the weaver among the Roman gods, <u>thought</u> she <u>is</u> the best weaver. She <u>considered</u> the materials she <u>wove</u> as beyond the capabilities of anyone else. But one day she <u>learns</u> about a simple peasant girl named Arachne who <u>is</u> also a very fine weaver. What really <u>outrages</u> Minerva <u>is</u> that Arachne <u>thought</u> her own work <u>was</u> superior.

So Minerva <u>challenges</u> Arachne to a weaving contest. Whoever <u>would create</u> the best work in the shortest amount of time <u>will be declared</u> the superior weaver. Arachne confidently <u>accepts</u> the challenge. They <u>set</u> up their looms side by side and <u>brought</u> in skeins and skeins of many colors of threads, even some gold and silver threads. It <u>is</u> like a rainbow in the room.

Then they <u>began</u> their work. Both weavers <u>worked</u> fast, efficiently, and very skillfully. When Minerva <u>finished</u>, she <u>has</u> a beautiful piece of cloth, but when she <u>looked</u> over at Arachne's piece, which Arachne <u>has</u> just completed at the same moment, Minerva <u>can see</u> that it <u>was</u> in no way inferior to hers. In a fit of anger, she <u>tears</u> Arachne's cloth from top to bottom and <u>began</u> beating Arachne about the head. Arachne <u>was</u> extremely angry at this treatment, but she <u>is</u> also disgraced because she <u>has been struck</u> by a deity. The result <u>was</u> that she <u>hangs</u> herself.

When Minerva <u>saw</u> what she <u>had done</u>, she <u>relents</u> and <u>takes</u> the body down. She <u>sprinkled</u> it with a certain magic liquid (known only to goddesses), which <u>changes</u> Arachne into a spider so she <u>could continue</u> to weave her beautiful webs. Of course, Minerva <u>is</u> left without any competition. <u>Do</u> you suppose she <u>thought</u> of that?

32 VERB TENSES: Conditional sentences and indirect quotations (22e)

The following sentences are conditional. From the choices in brackets, underline the appropriate form of each verb so that all verbs are in correct tense sequence.

Example: If more people got flu shots, fewer people [*will, would*] get sick.

1. Unless you get a flu shot, you (*may, would*) get the flu.

2. Every year when winter comes around, people [*were, are*] exposed to flu.

3. If you are allergic to eggs, you (*would, must, might*) have an allergic reaction to the flu shot.

4. If you get the flu after having a flu shot, your illness (*will be, was*) milder.

5. If you had had a flu shot last year, you (*might not have been, weren't*) so sick.

6. If you were not so afraid of shots, you (*will, would, did*) get a flu shot every year.

Change each direct quotation into an indirect quotation, deleting quotation marks and changing verbs as necessary so that they are in correct tense sequence. You will also have to change capital letters to lowercase and add *that* or *whether* before each indirect quotation. You may have to change *I* to *he* or *she*.

Example: Friedrich Nietzsche said, "Woman was God's second mistake."
Friedrich Nietzsche said that woman was God's second mistake.

7. William Faulkner said in his speech accepting the Nobel Prize, "I believe that man will not merely endure: he will prevail."

8. Cornelia Otis Skinner commented cynically, "Woman's virtue is man's greatest invention."

9. Even more cynical is Ogden Nash's statement: "Women would rather be right than reasonable."

10. Nietzsche also asked, "Is man only a blunder of God, or God only a blunder of man?"

33 MOOD OF VERBS: Subjunctive (23)

Below are the minutes of a fictional meeting. Complete the report by filling in an appropriate verb form wherever there is a blank space.

Example: The rules require that motions __be__ seconded.

Minutes of the Society for the Preservation of Garden Frog Ponds
August 31, 2000

The meeting of the Society for the Preservation of Garden Frog Ponds was called to order at 7:05 PM by the chair, Doris Francis, who urged that the assembled members _____ seated and _____ quiet. In the first item of business, Chair Francis recommended that she _____ appointed to examine the condition of the pond at Peabody Gardens. Its present condition suggests that it _____ removed from our list of Preserved Garden Frog Ponds. The assembled members moved and seconded the appointment and recommended that the chair _____ the pond from the list. The motion passed, and the chair thanked the members for their support.

Then Gordon Smythe stood up and informed the group about the pond at the home of Fred and Freddie Freeman. The elderly couple regrets the deteriorating condition of their pond, Smythe reported. If Freddie _____ in better health and if Fred _____ not broken his hip, they would be better able to care for the pond. Fred wishes he _____ stronger and more agile, said Smythe. Fred would have kept the pond in its former condition if he _____ been able. Cleo DeWitt suggested that the chair _____ a committee to care temporarily for the pond and that the committee _____ chaired by Smythe. Francis asked that DeWitt _____ her suggestion as a motion, which she did, and it was seconded by Smythe. The motion passed with one dissenting vote.

The meeting ended when the pizza arrived and everyone declared in unison, "We move that the meeting _____ adjourned!"

34 VOICE OF VERBS: Active vs. passive (24)

Rewrite the following passive sentences into active voice. You will have to add a new subject for some sentences.

> *Example:* Contaminants are removed from water at treatment plants.
> **Treatment plants remove contaminants from water.**

1. Water quality is determined by many factors.

2. Suspended and dissolved substances are contained in all natural waters.

3. The amounts of the substances are controlled by the environment.

4. Some dissolved substances are produced by pesticides.

5. Another element of quality is sediment that is deposited in water from fields, livestock feedlots, and other sources.

6. The bottom life of streams and lakes is affected by suspended sediment.

7. When light penetration is reduced by sediment, the life forms at the bottom may be smothered by the lack of light.

8. The quality of water in city systems is measured frequently at laboratories.

9. If legal levels are exceeded by pollutants, citizens must be notified by city officials.

10. The chlorine taste of city water is disliked by many people.

11. People think bottled water is safer, but a different taste is all that is purchased.

35 SUBJECT-VERB AGREEMENT: Intervening words, inverted order, and linking verbs (25b, i, j)

Decide whether the underlined words agree with their subjects. If a word is incorrect, cross it out and write the correct word above it.

Example: The shark, despite the beliefs of many people, ~~are~~ **is** beneficial to the sea environment.

One of the most feared creatures in the sea <u>are</u> sharks. These torpedo-shaped fish, which <u>lives</u> in nearly all seas of the world, <u>is</u> found in both shallow water and deep trenches. Some sharks <u>spend</u> most of their lives in a small, restricted area, while others <u>range</u> over wide distances.

There <u>is</u> a great variety in kinds of sharks. At one end of the scale <u>is</u> the tiny dwarf sharks, which <u>grows</u> to a length of four to six inches, and at the other end <u>is</u> the whale shark, which <u>reach</u> a length of forty-five feet. Sharks <u>differ</u> in appearance too. The hammerhead, which <u>has</u> a head shaped like a hammer, <u>has</u> eyes and nostrils at the ends of the hammer. The thresher shark <u>has</u> a long tail, and the angel shark <u>has</u> a flat body. There <u>is</u> also differences in the habits of sharks. They <u>swim</u> in schools or alone. They may be fast swimmers, or they may lurk on the bottom. The feature about sharks that most <u>worry</u> people <u>are</u> their aggressive natures. The fact <u>is</u> that some sharks <u>are</u> very aggressive, such as the great white, but others <u>take</u> little notice of a person in the water.

The skeleton of sharks is made up almost entirely of cartilage with only small amounts of bone. Even its spinal column is cartilage. Interestingly, scientists studying the shark has noticed that the spinal column provides a clue to a shark's age. One kind of shark, the lemon shark, develops rings on its spinal column, about thirteen a year, so scientists are able to guess the approximate age of this kind of shark. They have found that sharks live about one hundred years.

Because sharks take so many years to mature and is being slaughtered in huge numbers, they probably are not reproducing fast enough to keep their population intact.

36   SUBJECT-VERB AGREEMENT: Subjects with *and*; subjects with *or, nor* (25c,d)

In the following sentences, make the verbs agree with their subjects by underlining the correct form of each verb from the choices given in brackets.

Example: Business and household demand for credit [*is*, *are*] reduced during downturns in the economy.

1. Delayed capital investment or durable goods purchases [*has, have*] caused a depletion of inventory.

2. The purpose of the psychologist's investigation was to learn whether violence and strong language [*affects, affect*] children's behavior.

3. Technology, training, or capital provided by global companies actually [*limits, limit*] a country's potential.

4. A heart attack and mental exhaustion, not a promotion or a raise, [*is, are*] often the effect of workaholism.

5. A fifteen-year loan rather than a thirty-year loan greatly [*reduces, reduce*] interest expenses over the life of the loan.

6. Corporate restructuring and downsizing [*has, have*] been cited for detrimental effects on employee morale.

7. Studies show that pilots and the rest of the US population [*suffers, suffer*] from alcoholism at about the same rate.

8. Another study shows that bus drivers and truck drivers [*receives, receive*] better protection from the federal government than pilots do.

9. Improvement on the job and personal fulfillment [*results, result*] when the company employs a proven strategy of resolving problems.

10. Existing US labor practices and a cooperative approach [*is, are*] contrasted in the article.

37 SUBJECT-VERB AGREEMENT: Indefinite pronouns, collective nouns, singular nouns ending in -s, titles and defined words (25e,f,h,k)

Substitute the words in parentheses for the italicized subject(s) of each sentence. Then change the underlined verbs as necessary so that they agree with the new subjects.

Example: *All* of us <s>want</s> to become better at handwriting. (*None*)
                          None wants

1. *Most people* are a little unhappy about handwriting. (*Everyone*)

2. *All* of us have learned to write cursively; *none* of us is expert at it. (*Each one, all*)

3. *Anyone* is able to evaluate cursive writing by knowing just a few principles. (*Everyone*)

4. *Nothing* is more important than size in evaluating the quality of cursive. (*Slant and smoothness*)

5. *Some letters* use maximum height. (*Some handwriting*)

6. *This group* consists of all uppercase letters plus the lowercase letters *b, f, h, k,* and *l*. (*The letters in this group*)

7. *The largest group of* letters is the shortest in height: *a, c, e, g, m, n, o, q, r, s, u, v, w, x, y,* and *z*. (*Some*)

8. *All of the shortest letters* are half the size of the tallest letters. (*Each*)

9. The intermediate *group* consists of *d, i, u, p,* and *t*; they are three-fourths the size of the tall letters. (*letters*)

10. *A few letters* extend below the baseline: *f, g, j, p, q,* y, and *z*. (*Part of the alphabet*)

11. *These letters* are called descenders. (*The letters in this group*)

12. *Most people* never bother to evaluate the size and alignment of letters. (*Nobody*)

13. *Something* happens when we don't evaluate our handwriting: its quality deteriorates. (*Bad news*)

38   SUBJECT-VERB AGREEMENT: *Who, which, that* (25g)

Substitute the words in parentheses for the italicized words in each sentence. Then change the underlined verbs and other underlined words as necessary so that they agree with the new subjects.

Example:
           Job application letters   are   are
          The job application letter that <u>is</u> not proofread carefully <u>is</u> not likely to
                             applicants
          help <u>the applicant</u>. (*Job application letters*)

1. *Students* who <u>want</u> a good job after graduation <u>have</u> to begin preparing early for the job search. (*A student*)

2. *An aspect* of the job search that <u>requires</u> close attention <u>comes</u> when writing the application letter. (*Aspects*)

3. Two features of *application letters* that actually <u>reach</u> an employer's desk <u>are</u> conciseness and clarity. (*an application letter*)

4. The one feature of *application letters* that <u>appeals</u> most to employers <u>is</u> conciseness. (*the application letter*)

5. *The job applicant* who <u>wants</u> to have the best chance for an interview <u>reviews</u> the draft of the letter to get rid of unnecessary words. (*Job applicants*)

6. The employer will also be on the lookout for any potential *employee* who <u>sounds</u> sincerely interested but not overly eager. (*employees*)

7. *A student* who <u>hasn't</u> had much experience in the business world <u>finds</u> it difficult to strike the proper tone in the letter. (*Students*)

8. The *tone* that <u>makes</u> the best impression <u>is</u> matter-of-fact, sincere, and positive. (*style and tone*)

9. *A junior-level employee* who <u>is</u> willing to learn and to handle rather routine tasks <u>is</u> the type of person many employers are looking for. (*Junior-level employees*)

39   SUBJECT-VERB AGREEMENT: Review (25)

Rewrite the following paragraphs to describe "the Siberian tiger" (singular) instead of "Siberian tigers" (plural). Change verbs as necessary so that they agree with their new subjects. You will also have to change many pronouns from plural to singular. (See Chapter 27 of the handbook.)

First sentence: The Siberian tiger is the largest living cat in the world, much bigger than its relative the Bengal tiger.

Siberian tigers are the largest living cats in the world, much bigger than their relatives the Bengal tigers. They grow to a length of nine to twelve feet, including their tails, and to a height of about three and a half feet. They can weigh over six hundred pounds. These carnivorous hunters live in northern China and Korea as well as in Siberia. During the long winter of this Arctic climate, the yellowish striped coats get a little lighter in order to blend with the snow-covered landscape. The coats also grow quite thick, since the temperatures the tigers have to withstand can be as low as -50_ F.

Siberian tigers sometimes have to travel great distances to find food. They need about twenty pounds of food a day because of their size and the cold climate, but when they have fresh food they have been known to eat as much as a hundred pounds at one time. They hunt mainly deer, boars, and even bears, plus smaller prey such as fish and rabbits. They pounce on their prey and grab them by the back of the neck. Animals that aren't killed immediately are thrown to the ground and suffocated with a bite to the throat. Then the tigers feast.

Tiger cubs generally come in litters of three or four but sometimes as many as six. They stay with their mothers until they are three to five years old. When they are about six months old, they begin going out with their mothers on hunting trips. They begin hunting on their own when they are about a year old. At about two years, they are able to kill large prey.

Siberian tigers are an endangered subspecies. There may be as few as two hundred left in the wild, and about the same number can be counted in captivity.

40 IRREGULAR VERBS (21b)

For each sentence below, underline the correct form of the irregular verb from the choices given in brackets.

Example: The two workers have [hang, <u>hung</u>] plastic sheeting to cover the hole in the wall.

1. The water in the basement had [risen, rose] to nearly a foot by the morning after last week's storm.

2. Our neighbors, the Hills, had a sump pump [setting, sitting] in the corner of their basement, but it wasn't working because of the power failure.

3. After a massive thunderstorm hit the area, many power lines were damaged by trees that had [fallen, fell] down.

4. The morning after the storm, a huge oak tree was found [laying, lying] on the power line at the end of our neighbor's driveway.

5. When we went to check on them, they were busy [setting, sitting] sand bags around the edge of their basement.

6. They had been up all night and had hardly had a chance to [lay, lie] down.

7. As soon as they [sat, set] down to rest, the power came back on.

8. The tree [lay, laid] on the power line for most of the day before it was removed.

9. We have had several charitable activities to benefit victims of the storm, and so far have [raised, risen, rose] $5,000.

10. We have [sat, set] a long-term goal of $10,000.

41   PRONOUN CASE (26a,b,d)

Substitute the appropriate pronoun for each underlined noun.

Example: <u>Twain</u> and his family moved to Europe in 1891.   **He**

1. <u>Mark Twain's</u> real name was Samuel Langhorne Clemens.

2. It was <u>Mark Twain</u> who wrote *The Adventures of Huckleberry Finn*.

3. <u>Twain</u> and his brother Orion published a local newspaper.

4. Orion asked <u>Twain</u> to write for the paper.

5. The newspaper was the first business venture for <u>Twain</u> and Orion.

6. Later the two men, <u>Twain</u> and Orion, went to Carson City, Nevada.

7. The work they did there was different for the two men, for <u>Twain</u> and his brother.

8. His brother became territorial secretary, and <u>Twain</u> himself wrote for the newspaper there.

9. Probably no one enjoyed writing more than <u>Twain</u>.

10. It was in Carson City, in 1863, that it occurred to <u>Twain</u> to write under the name Mark Twain.

11. <u>Twain's</u> changing his name derived from his years on the Mississippi, when the steamboat's leadsman would call out "mark twain," meaning two fathoms, or safe water.

12. <u>Twain</u> achieved renown as an author in 1865 with <u>Twain's</u> story "The Celebrated Jumping Frog of Calaveras County."

13. In 1870, <u>Mark Twain</u> and Olivia Langdon were married in Elmira, New York.

14. In the next year, Hartford, Connecticut, became the home for <u>Mark</u> and Olivia.

15. There, <u>Twain</u> the journalist became the literary writer.

16. *Roughing It*, written in 1872, tells of the years <u>Twain</u> and Orion spent in the West.

17. <u>Twain's</u> masterpiece, *The Adventures of Huckleberry Finn*, won accolades for <u>Twain</u>, the literary writer.

42   PRONOUN CASE: *Who, whom* (26c)

Rewrite the following statements as questions, substituting *who* or *whom* for the underlined words.

Example: Jacques Cartier sailed the St. Lawrence River as far as the modern site of Montreal.
Who sailed the St. Lawrence River as far as the modern site of Montreal?

1. Jacques Cartier explored the St. Lawrence region of Quebec in 1534-35.

2. A trading post was built by Samuel de Champlain in 1608 on the site of Quebec City.

3. Lake Champlain in New York was named for Champlain.

4. In the Quebec Act of 1774, the British granted the region the right to retain its French language and institutions.

Combine each pair of statements into a single sentence, replacing the underlined word(s) with *who* or *whom*.

Example: Jacques Cartier was an important explorer in Canada.
French claims to the St. Lawrence valley were based on him.
Jacques Cartier, on whom French claims to the St. Lawrence were based, was an important explorer in Canada.

5. Samuel de Champlain was a French explorer.
He was the chief founder of New France.

6. Much of eastern Canada was explored by Champlain.
He went as far west as Lakes Huron and Ontario and south into New York.

7. Quebec was settled by his colonists.
He brought his colonists there in 1608.

8. Champlain was an important early figure in Canada.
Port Royal, Nova Scotia, was founded by him.

43 PRONOUN-ANTECEDENT AGREEMENT I (27)

Make pronouns agree with their antecedents by underlining the correct form from the choices in brackets. Avoid the generic *he* with the indefinite pronouns.

Example: How can you protect [*yourself*, oneself, ourselves] from sun damage to the skin?

1. Researchers and physicians have repeatedly sounded [*their*, his, his or her] warnings about the dangers of tanning.

2. Everyone should be aware that tanning can have serious consequences for [their, his, *his or her*] long-term health.

3. Some people think that [*they*, we] can tan safely.

4. But doctors tell us that [they, *we*] know of no safe tanning.

5. No one can get a tan that is totally safe for [their, his, *his or her*] skin.

6. Some people use tanning lamps because they think [*they're*, it's] less risky.

7. But any researcher would repeat [their, his, *his or her*] warning that lamps may be more dangerous than sunlight because [*they*, it]) can allow ultraviolet (UV) rays to penetrate more deeply.

8. Exposure to UV light may cause a person to develop premature aging of [their, *his or her*, our] skin.

9. One may also encounter an even more serious consequence: the development of cancer on [their, his or her, *one's*] skin.

10. It is a statistical fact that nearly every case of skin cancer had UV exposure as [their, *its*] cause.

11. Light-skinned people or any other person who burns easily would be especially at risk of developing UV damage to [their, *his or her*] skin.

12. People who need to spend time in the sun can protect [*themselves*, themself, oneself] by using sunscreen and covering up with loose-fitting clothing.

44   PRONOUN-ANTECEDENT AGREEMENT II (27)

In each blank space, add a pronoun that contributes to the meaning of the passage, making sure that the pronoun agrees with its antecedent.

Example: Polar bears are excellent swimmers, using **their** front legs to propel **them** through the water.

Picture a polar bear prowling about five miles away on _____ natural landscape of snow and ice. Using your binoculars, can you see _____ looking at you? What _____ need to look for is the black spot that is _____ nose. People say that polar bears are likely to cover the nose when stalking seals because _____ can be seen so well in the white polar world.

This great white bear stands about five feet to _____ shoulders, and on _____ hind legs can be as tall as eleven feet. _____ is the largest of the bear family. The feet on this bear are about twelve inches long, and _____ are covered with fur, even on _____ soles. These bears weigh up to a thousand pounds. Each bear may live _____ life in solitude. They come together mainly to mate, although sometimes _____ feed in groups. A group of polar bears may feed on _____ find of carrion or freshly killed seals, walrus, or land animals.

A mother polar bear and _____ cubs spend _____ winter months in a den that _____ has dug in the snow. The den can be as much as forty degrees warmer than the outside air. When born, the cubs are about the size of rats, and _____ are hairless, blind, and deaf. The cubs and _____ mother emerge from _____ den in March or April, but _____ continue under _____ care until _____ are three years old. Each one can then begin _____ life as an independent adult.

45   PRONOUN REFERENCE I (28)

Make each underlined pronoun below refer clearly to its antecedent, or rewrite the sentence to eliminate the confusing reference.

Example: To remove all obstacles for people with disabilities, it requires a change in attitudes.
To remove all obstacles for people with disabilities requires a change in attitudes.

1. The university's attitude toward students with disabilities is evident in the inadequacy of the accessibility it has provided.

2. Before we can improve current conditions for students with disabilities, we must learn where they are.

3. One of the first places to investigate is the cramped office of Disabilities Services. This would allow us to locate the center of the problem.

4. In the Americans with Disabilities Act of 1990, it calls for "reasonable accommodation."

5. This means that essential facilities must be easily available and functional.

6. On this campus you can easily find violations of the law.

7. The Disabilities Services office is a prime example of this.

8. Formerly a store room, the office doesn't have a doorway wide enough for you to get a wheelchair through.

9. The ramp at one building hardly allows access to it.

10. Yet the Disabilities Service office provides services, such as sign-language interpreters and note takers if you have a recognized disability.

46 PRONOUN REFERENCE II (28)

Some of the underlined pronouns in the following paragraphs do not refer clearly to their antecedents or are inconsistent from sentence to sentence. Revise the paragraphs as necessary, making pronoun references clear when possible, rewriting to eliminate confusing references, and resolving inconsistencies.

Example: In the thank-you letter, <u>it</u> conveys appreciation for <u>their</u> time.
The thank-you letter conveys appreciation for the interviewer's time.

Some students prepare for work in a chosen field by arranging an informational interview with someone <u>who</u> works in <u>it</u>. <u>This</u> gives a student the advantage of making <u>you</u> more knowledgeable about <u>it</u> and helps <u>you</u> clarify career goals. The interview is also an excellent way for the student to establish a network of contacts <u>that</u> can lead to future employment.

To set up the informational interview, <u>it</u> involves first doing some research about the occupational field. If <u>this</u> is what <u>you</u> want to do, use the career counseling services at <u>your</u> school to learn the job titles and job requirements in that field. Then identify career professionals in <u>it</u> <u>who</u> are knowledgeable in the targeted jobs or organizations. Telephone or write <u>them</u> to set up appointments. If <u>they</u> are too busy to meet with you, thank <u>them</u> and ask if <u>they</u> can name someone else <u>who</u> might agree to an interview.

Prepare for the interview by studying the organization: <u>its</u> annual reports, brochures, and so on. Think about what you can ask <u>them</u>, and make a list of the questions you want answered. In your list <u>it</u> might include such questions as "What is your typical workweek like?" and "What are the most rewarding aspects of the job?" You might also want to know what credentials, degrees, or licenses <u>it</u> requires. <u>That</u> may lead to questions about how job openings are advertised and how many people <u>it</u> hires in a year.

If you do decide to do <u>this</u>, remember that <u>it</u> is not a job interview. You are meeting with <u>them</u> for the purpose of information only. If <u>they</u> happen to ask you about your experience and educational background, take advantage of <u>this</u> and let <u>them</u> know about your strengths and interests. Take a résumé with you, just in case <u>they</u> ask to see it.

47 PRONOUNS: Review (26, 27, 28)

Underline the correct pronoun choice from the items in brackets.

Example: Each of the people in the homeless shelter received help in filling out [his or her, their] application for assistance.

When Jim and Kirsten volunteered at the local homeless shelter, they did [his or her, their] best to help the people visiting the shelter. Kirsten distributed blankets because she hoped [it, they] would keep people warm. Jim's old truck did [its, her] best to carry cartons from the food bank to the shelter. Each person who worked with Jim felt [his or her, their] life enriched by the experience. Each of the volunteers had [his or her, their] own reason for working at the shelter. For Jim and Kirsten, the reasons were related to [their, his and her] early life. As Jim explained, "Kirsten and [I, me, myself] spent many of our early years in shelters. It is important to [her and me, she and I, her and myself] to give something back to the community."

48 ADJECTIVES AND ADVERBS (29)

Underline the appropriate form of each modifier from the choices given in brackets.

Example: Thunderstorms are more numerous in Tampa, Florida, than [*Santa Fe, New Mexico; in Santa Fe, New Mexico*].

1. You may be able to predict the weather if you study the clouds [*serious, seriously*].

2. Knowing the clouds is at least [*more better, better*] than guessing the weather.

3. The cumulonimbus is probably more familiar than [*any, any other*] cloud.

4. Seeing this cloud, a person could [*hardly, not hardly*] avoid forecasting a storm.

5. The rain will probably fall [*heavy, heavily*], and lightning will crack.

6. Without the "nimbus" in its name, the cumulus cloud [*usual, usually*] denotes fair weather.

7. These clouds are the fluffy, cotton-ball type that we see on [*more sunny, sunnier*] days.

8. The shape of stratus clouds is different from [*cumulus clouds, that of cumulus clouds*].

9. Stratus clouds spread out [*uniformly, uniform*] in an indefinite shape.

10. A type of stratus cloud, the altostratus, tells us that rain is coming when the sky looks [*darkly, dark*] in the west.

11. When rain falls [*heavy, heavily*] from the altostratus, it becomes a nimbostratus.

12. Cirrus clouds are higher in the sky than [*any, any other*] clouds.

13. Cirrus clouds develop at altitudes exceeding 20,000 feet and are [*most always, always*] made up of ice crystals.

14. They might take the shape of paint brushes or commas, and they seem to move [*slow, slowly*].

15. When cirrus clouds are overhead, the weather will be [*fair, fairly*].

16. But they are often followed by the [*more lower and darker, lower and darker*] altostratus rain clouds.

49   ADJECTIVES (29)

Underline the appropriate form of each modifier from the choices given in brackets.

Example: Of the two candy bars—Snickers and Baby Ruth—which is the [<u>older</u>, oldest]?

1. I thought the orchestra played [good, <u>well</u>], though my friends didn't agree.

2. The violinists seemed to take their work [serious, <u>seriously</u>].

3. Just because a piece of music sounds [<u>good</u>, well] does not mean it is worth careful study.

4. The careers of many musicians are going [bad, <u>badly</u>].

5. One group's most recent CD sold [<u>better</u>, more better, more well] in England than in the United States.

6. The record company found some [real, <u>really</u>] surprising trends when they conducted marketing research.

7. The group's CDs were selling [good, <u>well</u>] among customers over 40 and customers under 18.

8. However, sales to customers in the 19-39 age range were doing [poor, <u>poorly</u>].

9. The marketing experts were at a loss to explain why one group would appeal to two audiences that are so [<u>wide</u>, widely] apart.

10. If you listen [close, <u>closely</u>] to the CD, you will hear the sound of a children's choir in the background.

50 ORDER OF ADJECTIVES I (29, 30a)

A series of adjectives is given after each sentence. Place the adjectives in the correct sequence for the position indicated by the blank line.

Example: A _____ diner opened on Route 5. (Greek, new)

Answer: A **new Greek** diner opened on Route 5.

1. A _____ diner on Route 5 is one of the most popular gathering places for young people in the area. (*crowded, small*)

2. Unlike many fast-food restaurants, the diner features _____ salads. (*fresh, green*)

3. One of their _____ items is a chocolate malt. (*menu, most popular, new*)

4. It is served in a _____ cup with both a straw and a spoon. (*large, silver*)

5. Some of the _____ students go to the diner on Friday afternoons. (*high-school, local, popular*)

6. They order malts and French fries and then play classic rock-and-roll records on the _____ jukebox. (*antique, large*)

7. On Saturdays, shoppers on their way to the mall stop in for the diner's _____ breakfast special: bagel and coffee. (*fast, inexpensive*)

8. Sunday tends to be family day, with _____ children running down the aisles while their families wait for their food. (*little, numerous, noisy*)

9. On Monday, the diner is closed so that the _____ family who owns it can catch their breath before another busy week begins. (*Greek, small*)

10. On Tuesday, the diner re-opens, and by 7:30 a.m. the booths are filled with _____ residents ordering breakfast. (*hungry, local*)

51 ORDER OF ADJECTIVES II (29, 30a)

A group of adjectives follows each sentence below. Rearrange the adjectives as needed for appropriate order in English, and write them in that order on the blank spaces provided.

Example: Computer graphics perform __many__ __tedious__ __drafting__ chores.
(*drafting many tedious*)

1. _____ _____ _____ _____ specialist developed image controls. (*computer a Chinese young*)

2. _____ _____ _____ _____ engineer assisted him. (*a American skeptical electrical*)

3. _____ _____ _____ researchers are carrying out further study. (*engineering several university*)

4. The controls depend on _____ _____ _____ object connected by wires to the computer. (*T-shaped hand-sized a*).

5. The image allows a biochemist to walk into _____ _____ _____ display of a molecule. (*holographic gigantic a*)

6. Using _____ _____ gestures, the biochemist can rotate and change the entire image. (*simple hand*)

7. _____ _____ _____ games also depend on computer graphics. (*computer all video*)

8. Even _____ _____ _____ games operate this way. (*sophisticated simulation flight*)

9. One game is played with _____ _____ _____ racquets. (*rectangular thin two*)

10. In the early years of computers, scientists made _____ _____ _____ drawings to simulate motion. (*crude some animated*)

52 ADJECTIVES AND ADVERBS: Determiners (29f)

Underline the appropriate article from the choices given in brackets. If no article is needed, choose *0*.

Example: [*The*, *A*, *0*] least windy place in [*the*, *0*] United States is [*the*, *0*] Roseburg, Oregon.

1. Meteorologists have named many kinds of [*a, the, 0*] wind.

2. They have named [*a, the, 0*] chinook and [*a, the, 0*] tornado.

3. [*The, 0*] winds may blow away the snow on [*your, 0*] roof, or they may blow away [*your, 0*] roof.

4. The winds of [*a, 0*] hurricane can do great damage.

5. They can blow down [*the, a, 0*] trees and houses.

6. [*The, A, 0*] winds of [*the, an, 0*] hurricane are matched by those of [*the, 0*] tornado.

7. [*A, 0*] tornado is [*a, the, 0*] whirling funnel-shaped cloud that contains [*the, 0*] winds of 150 miles [*a, an, the, 0*] hour or more.

8. There are stories of [*a, 0*] piece of [*the, 0*] straw driven into [*a, the, 0*] board and of [*a, 0*] bean embedded in [*a, an, the, 0*] egg.

9. [*The, 0*] Chicago has [*the, a, an, 0*] reputation for being [*the, a, an, 0*] windy city.

10. It is windy because of [*the, a, 0*] Lake Michigan to [*the, 0*] northeast and [*the, 0*] Great Plains to the west and south.

11. But there are [*the, 0*] windier cities, such as Miami, New York, and Wichita.

12. [*The, A, 0*] windiest place in [*the, 0*] United States is Mount Washington, New Hampshire, where [*a, the, 0*] gust of 231 miles [*a, an, the, 0*] hour was recorded.

13. In general, [*the, 0*] winds blow faster in [*a, 0*] winter than in [*a, 0*] summer.

14. And in [*the, 0*] United States they generally blow from [*the, a, 0*] west.

53 ADJECTIVES AND ADVERBS: Present and past participles (29e)

Underline the appropriate participle from the choices given in brackets.

Example: Is it so [*astonishing*, *astonished*] that a person should enjoy a lecture?

1. Yesterday I attended an [*interesting*, *interested*] lecture on microeconomics.

2. I was actually [*surprising*, *surprised*] at my interest.

3. I fully expected the lecture to be [*boring*, *bored*].

4. I was [*pleasing*, *pleased*] to find it so [*fascinating*, *fascinated*].

5. I was so [*exciting*, *excited*] at what the lecturer was saying that by the end of the lecture I was [*exhausting*, *exhausted*].

6. My friends think it is [*amusing*, *amused*] that I enjoyed the lecture.

7. They seem to think I should be [*embarrassing*, *embarrassed*] about my excitement over microeconomics.

8. But I am [*confusing*, *confused*] about their attitude.

9. Should a person be [*surprising*, *surprised*] to find learning [*satisfying*, *satisfied*]?

10. I was getting [*annoying*, *annoyed*] at my friends because of their attitude.

11. I was also getting [*tiring*, *tired*] of their taunts.

12. You might say that I was finding them [*tiring*, *tired*].

13. In the end, I found the whole scene very [*amusing*, *amused*].

54 MISPLACED MODIFIERS (30a)

Complete each sentence by indicating with a _ mark where the italicized word or phrase should be placed and writing the word in above the mark.

Example: Writing is _ the same for right-handers and left-handers. (*hardly*) — **hardly**

1. We live in a right-handed society. (*largely*)

2. Hand tools, machines, and doors are designed for right-handed people. (*even*)

3. However, 15 percent of the population may be left-handed. (*nearly*)

4. When children begin school, they may prefer one hand or the other. (*already*)

5. If the preferred hand is the left, it's better for the teacher not to try to change that preference. (*intentionally*)

6. The teacher should teach right-handed writing when the child is right-handed or ambidextrous. (*only*)

7. If the child seems to have a preference, the teacher can test for true ambidexterity. (*not*)

8. The teacher can observe the child's picking up or using various materials. (*and keep a record of*)

9. The child can pick up a key or hammer nails. (*simply*)

10. If the child indicates true ambidexterity, it is better to train the right hand. (*probably*)

11. One problem that left-handers have is reversing the lowercase *d* and *b* and the *p* and *q*. (*commonly*; *when writing*)

12. Teachers can demonstrate to the right-handers and the left-handers how to set the paper. (*both*)

55   DANGLING MODIFIERS (30b)

The following sentences are taken from several student papers. Revise the sentences so that each underlined modifier clearly modifies the word it is intended to modify. You will have to add, delete, and rearrange words.

    Example: <u>Although not invited to speak at the conference,</u> Peck's address excited the conferees.
                  Although Peck was not invited to speak at the conference, his address excited the conferees.
    or   Although not invited to speak at the conference, Peck excited the conferees with his address.

1. <u>Though actively involved in volunteer organizations,</u> Ed's résumé shows only how productive he has been in our company.

2. <u>After receiving the final notice on November 9,</u> all correspondence regarding this order ceased.

3. <u>Being a college student,</u> three weeks without my computer was a long time.

4. <u>Having spoken to one of your associates,</u> payment arrangements were made.

5. <u>To greatly reduce the interest you will pay,</u> it is suggested that you choose a fifteen-year loan.

6. <u>After receiving a loan for $8,000 from a relative,</u> the house cost Mike and Sally $50,000.

7. <u>To be sure you have all the parts before you start,</u> the parts list should first be checked.

8. <u>In addition to using reason,</u> intuition helps people solve problems.

9. <u>If interested in reading the entire article,</u> it can be found in the most recent issue of the journal.

10. <u>To make a donation to the youth camp,</u> it can be sent to the committee chairperson.

56   FRAGMENTS I (31)

The list below contains both complete sentences and sentence fragments. Apply the tests for fragments: (1) underline every verb twice, (2) underline every subject once, and (3) put brackets around any subordinating conjunctions or relative pronouns. Then revise any fragments so that they are complete sentences.

Example: Visitors to Washington, DC, tour the Mall. [Which] contains many of the city's attractions.
Visitors to Washington, DC, tour the Mall, which contains many of the city's attractions.

1. If you visit Washington, DC, you should be sure to tour several places.

2. One is the national Air and Space Museum.

3. To avoid the heaviest crowds, go early.

4. Just inside the lobby, the Wright brothers' plane and Lindbergh's *Spirit of St. Louis.*

5. One of the busiest areas is Space Hall. Where you can tour Skylab.

6. An informative one-hour guided tour costing you nothing.

7. Another place to see being the National Museum of American History. Many people's favorite museum.

8. It offers something for everybody.

9. A Model-T Ford and other vintage automobiles, steam locomotives, farm equipment, and evening gowns worn by some of the Presidents' wives.

10. And you can get lunch in the cafeteria.

11. One of the new museums being the US Holocaust Memorial Museum. Established in 1993.

12. Not for the faint-hearted. Audio-visual displays show the horrors of the Nazi persecution.

57   FRAGMENTS II (31)

Revise each sentence fragment in the following paragraphs by attaching it to a sentence or rewriting it as a complete sentence.

Example: Gymnosperms, the most advanced of nonflowering plants. They thrive in diverse environments.
Gymnosperms, the most advanced of nonflowering plants, thrive in diverse environments.

People generally avoid eating mushrooms except those they buy in stores. But as a matter of fact many varieties of mushrooms are edible. Mushrooms are members of a large group of vegetation called nonflowering plants. Including algae, mosses, ferns, and coniferous trees. Even the giant redwoods of California. Most of the nonflowering plants prefer moist environments. Such as forest floors, fallen timber, and still water. Mushrooms, for example, prefer moist, shady soil. Algae grow in water.

Most mushrooms, both edible and inedible, are members of a class called basidium fungi. A term referring to their method of reproduction. The basidia produce spores. Which can develop into mushrooms. This classification including the prized meadow mushroom, cultivated commercially, and the amanitas. The amanita group contains both edible and poisonous species. Another familiar group of mushrooms, the puffballs. They are easily identified by their round shape. Their spores are contained under a thick skin. Which eventually ruptures to release the spores. The famous morels are in still another group. These pitted, spongy mushrooms called sac fungi because the spores develop in sacs.

Anyone interested in mushrooms as food should heed the US Public Health Service warning. To not eat any wild mushrooms unless their identity and edibility are established without a doubt.

58 COMMA SPLICES AND FUSED SENTENCES: *and, but,* etc.
(32a)

The following compound sentences are correct as written and punctuated. Write sentences of your own that match the given sentences in linking main clauses with a semicolon alone or with a comma and a coordinating conjunction.

> *Example:*   The Mississippi River drains the nation; its tributaries reach to the west, to the north, and to the east.
> Computers serve the business world; their benefits touch retailers, industry, and service organizations.

1. The Mississippi River begins in Lake Itasca in Minnesota, and it flows south for 2,348 miles to the Gulf of Mexico.

2. Five states line its east bank, and five states line its west bank.

3. The upper Mississippi has several important tributaries; among them are the Illinois, Chippewa, Black, Wisconsin, Saint Croix, Iowa, Des Moines, and Rock rivers.

4. The Missouri River is by far the largest tributary; it is the longest one and contributes a tremendous amount of water and sediment drained from the Great Plains.

5. Another major tributary, the Ohio River, enters the Mississippi at Cairo, Illinois, and it contributes drainage from the area east to the Appalachians.

6. Cairo, Illinois, marks the beginning of the lower Mississippi valley; this flat sedimentary area was once an extension of the Gulf of Mexico.

7. The river has been depositing sediment for thousands of years; scientists estimate the amount to be approximately 1,280 cubic miles.

8. The river has created natural levees from deposited sediment, but even so it has caused devastating floods.

9. To prevent floods, the federal government has built huge artificial levees and dredged channels, but the river continues to create problems.

10. It is navigable from Minneapolis to the Gulf, but the channel is deeper on the lower Mississippi than on the upper river.

59   COMMA SPLICES AND FUSED SENTENCES: *however*, etc.
(32b)

Combine each of the following pairs of sentences into a single sentence with two main clauses. Relate the main clauses with a semicolon and a conjunctive adverb or transitional expression. (Consult the list in 32b of the handbook if you need help with your selection.) Match the example below in placing a comma after the adverb or expression.

Example: Turtles do not chew their food.
They swallow it in chunks.
Turtles do not chew their food; instead, they swallow it in chunks.

1. Some people think that dinosaurs were the first living vertebrates.
Fossils of turtles go back 40 million years further.

2. Turtles are reptiles with a bony, body-encasing shell.
They are essentially the same as they were 200 million years ago.

3. Turtles inhabit a variety of environments worldwide.
Most other reptiles exist mainly in tropical regions.

4. In size, turtles range from about four inches to eight feet long.
An extinct sea turtle reached a length of nearly twelve feet.

5. Turtles do not have teeth.
Their jaws are covered with a sharp, horny sheath.

6. A turtle's ribs and backbone are attached to its rigid upper shell.
Its skeletal limb-support system is located within the rib cage.

7. Turtles cannot expand their lungs to breathe air.
They make adjustments in how space is used within the shell.

8. Some turtles can get oxygen from water.
They don't need to breathe air.

9. Both upper and lower shells are covered with a thin layer of skin.
The skin is covered with a layer of horny scales.

10. Turtles are able to shut down their metabolism.
They hibernate during cold weather.

60 COMMA SPLICES AND FUSED SENTENCES: Review (32)

Correct comma splices and fused sentences in the following paragraphs by making new sentences, adding coordinating conjunctions, replacing commas with semicolons, or making main clauses into subordinate structures.

Example: Armenia became the first Christian nation in AD 300, its king adopted Christianity for his kingdom.
Armenia became the first Christian nation in AD 300 when its king adopted Christianity for his kingdom.

What is known as the first genocide of modern times occurred during World War I, the Armenians were deported from their homes in Anatolia. The Turkish government assumed that the Armenians were sympathetic to Russia, with whom the Turks were at war. Many Armenians died because of the hardships of the journey, many were massacred. The death toll was estimated at between 600,000 and a million.

Many of the deported Armenians migrated to Russia, in 1918 they established the Republic of Armenia, they continued to be under attack by Turkey, in 1920 they became the Soviet Republic of Armenia rather than surrender to the Turks. Like other Soviet republics, Armenia became independent in 1991, about 3.4 million Armenians live there now. Approximately the same number is dispersed to other countries.

The Armenians have a long history of conquest by other nations. As a people, they migrated to Armenia in the seventh century BC, being ruled then by the Persian empire until it was conquered by Alexander the Great. Then followed Greek and Roman rule, then internal clan leadership marked by disunity and strife. In 640 the country was invaded by the Arabs in the eleventh century it was conquered by the Byzantines and later by the Turks, under whose control it remained.

Conflict for the Armenians continues it has territorial disputes with its neighbor Azerbaijan. Many Armenians have settled in Azerbaijan.

61 MIXED SENTENCES (33a,b)

Revise the following sentences so that subjects and predicates match in meaning and in grammar.

Example: In studying economics has two parts: microeconomics and macroeconomics.
Economics has two parts: microeconomics and macroeconomics.

1. Microeconomics is where the economic behavior of individual units is studied.

2. By studying individual consumers and firms is a way to learn alternative means of production.

3. The use of microeconomics also helps firms to make decisions about pricing their products.

4. Microeconomics, as a branch of economics, is the definition of how individual resources are allocated to satisfy human wants.

5. Economic resources are the use of things or services that produce goods.

6. With the traditional classification of economic resources as land, labor, and capital has a limited usage today.

7. The reason for this change in usage is because each of these resources has branched out into so many varieties.

8. Because of the limitations of existing technology result in limitations on economics.

9. Microeconomics is also where the workings of the price system are studied.

10. By understanding the price system helps to answer questions about prices of commodities, wages of workers, and so on.

62 MIXED SENTENCES: Repeated subjects and other parts (33c)

Draw a line through any pronouns or other words that are not needed in the following sentences.

Example: Scientists ~~they~~ use special instruments for measuring the age of artifacts.

1. Archaeologists and other scientists ~~they~~ can often determine the age of their discoveries by means of radiocarbon dating.

2. This technique ~~it~~ can be used on any material that once was living.

3. The technique is based on the fact that all living organisms ~~they~~ contain carbon.

4. Scientists call this common isotope carbon 12, which ~~it~~ contains 6 protons and 6 neutrons.

5. A few carbon atoms are classified as the isotope carbon 14, where there is a nucleus of 6 protons and 8 neutrons ~~there~~.

6. Because of the extra neutrons, the carbon 14 atom ~~it~~ is unstable and radioactive.

7. What is significant about the carbon 14 atom ~~it~~ is its half life of 5,700 years.

8. The half life means that in every 5,700 years half of the carbon 14 in a specimen ~~it~~ will decay.

9. So scientists ~~they~~ measure the proportion of carbon 14 to carbon 12 and estimate the age of the specimen.

10. This kind of dating is most accurate when a specimen is between 500 and 50,000 years old ~~then~~.

11. With younger specimens, too little carbon 14 has decayed, and with older ones too little is left that the scientists can measure ~~it~~.

63 END PUNCTUATION (34)

Insert end punctuation marks wherever they are needed in the following sentences.

Example: Is privacy any less common today than it was back when everybody lived in small towns and knew everybody else's business
Is privacy any less common today than it was back when everybody lived in small towns and knew everybody else's business?

1. Yesterday I decided to order a CD album from a mail-order company

2. The person taking the telephone order asked, "What is your zip code"

3. Then she asked me what the rest of my address was

4. I told her my PO box address in Greenville, NC

5. Next she asked what my customer number was

6. Finally, I asked her, "Don't you want to know my name"

7. She answered, "I already know your name, Mr Bronson It's in the computer"

8. All I could say was an emphatic "Oh"

9. I wondered, though, how my name got into the computer

10. Then I asked myself, "How many other computers is my name in"

11. "And what else about me is in those computers" I wondered

12. And I wanted to know where those computers got that information

13. Then I began thinking about how much the bank, the US government, and my credit card company know about me

14. I started getting paranoid and wondered if ESPN had me in its computer–or *USA Today* or even, and here I was really getting wild, the H J Heinz Company

15. But my fantasizing came to an abrupt halt when the person on the telephone shouted, "Sir Sir Your order please"

16. "Never mind," I said "There's no order after all"

64   COMMA: With coordinating conjunctions and introductory elements (35a,b)

Insert commas in the following paragraphs where they are needed between main clauses joined by coordinating conjunctions (*and, but, or, nor, for, so, yet*) or to set off introductory elements.

Example: Estimating wind speed is easy and most people can make a guess.
Estimating wind speed is easy**,** and most people can make a guess.

Most people have more knowledge than they are aware of when it comes to predicting the weather and meteorologists don't seem to mind having the layperson dabble in forecasting. In fact they will often help. One indication of weather is wind speed but most of us are not any more scientific about it than knowing that the day is windy or very windy. However meteorologists define winds by their effects.

They begin with a calm wind or you might say no wind. In this category smoke rises straight up and leaves on trees do not move. At the next level light air is described by a slight drift of smoke and leaves barely moving. Its speed is 1 to 3 miles per hour. Next come five levels termed breezes that range from 4 to 31 miles an hour. With a light breeze you can feel the wind on your face and the leaves on trees move slightly. The gentle breeze blows a little faster and puts leaves and twigs in constant motion. The moderate breeze blows 13 to 18 miles per hour and moves small branches. In a fresh breeze small trees sway and clouds of dust can blow up. The strong breeze is a 25- to 31-mile-per-hour wind and puts large branches in motion.

Gales can begin to be destructive and inconvenient. Blowing at 32 to 38 miles per hour the moderate gale sets whole trees moving. With a fresh gale twigs break off trees and walking is difficult. At 47 to 54 miles per hour the strong gale causes slight structural damage so chimneys and roof shingles may blow off. The whole gale seldom occurs inland but when it does it uproots trees and causes considerable structural damage.

The last two categories occur only rarely. What the meteorologists term a storm blows at 64 to 74 miles per hour and causes widespread damage and a hurricane wind blowing at over 75 miles per hour brings about excessive destruction.

65 COMMA: With nonessential elements (35c)

At the _ mark in each sentence below, insert the phrases given in parentheses. Then add commas as needed to set off any of these added elements that are nonessential.

Example: The alligator _ spends its life in or near water. (*an amphibious reptile*)
The alligator, **an amphibious reptile**, spends its life in or near water.

1. The American alligator's range is limited to the southeastern states _ . (*mainly Florida*)

2. Georgia and Alabama _ have native alligators. (*in addition to Florida*)

3. A relative _ inhabits the same areas. (*the American crocodile*)

4. The crocodile _ is slightly smaller and has a narrower snout. (*which looks much like the alligator*)

5. The alligator is about thirteen feet long _ . (*its tail accounting for half its length*)

6. Alligators eat almost anything that comes close enough to be caught _ . (*such as small mammals and fish*).

7. Such small prey _ are swallowed whole. (*which are quickly snapped up*)

8. Larger mammals are usually dragged under water and drowned _ . (*before being torn into pieces and swallowed*)

9. Alligators _ came close to extinction. (*once widely hunted for their skin*)

10. A conservation program _ saved them from becoming extinct. (*that was set up in the 1950s*)

11. Anyone _ can view them at one of the alligator farms in the southeastern United States. (*wanting to see real live alligators*)

66 COMMA: With items in series; two or more adjectives; dates, addresses, place names, long numbers; *she said*, etc. (35d,e,f,g)

At the _ mark in the following sentences, insert the words given in parentheses. Then add commas where necessary. You may also have to change capitalization or add quotation marks.

Example: The most popular dogs in the United States appear to be the Labrador retriever _ and the German shepherd. (*the Rottweiler*)
The most popular dogs in the United States appear to be the Labrador retriever, the Rottweiler, and the German shepherd.

1. _ "None so blind as those who will not see." (*Matthew Henry said*)

2. Among winners of the Nobel Prize for literature are Seamus Henry _ and Toni Morrison. (*Joseph Brodsky*)

3. The layers of the skin are epidermis _ and subcutaneous tissue. (*dermis*)

4. The rose _ and gold corals are like dazzling underwater flowers. (*green*)

5. It was early on October 14 _ that a military coup ousted the prime minister. (*1994*)

6. Spokane _ is where you'll find Gonzaga University. (*Washington*)

7. _ "No matter how thin you slice it, it's still baloney." (*Politician Alfred Emanuel Smith is credited with saying*)

8. "The whole of science _ is nothing more than a refinement of everyday thinking." (*said Albert Einstein*)

9. Corals produce colorful _ and often delicate structures. (*beautifully shaped*)

10. January 7 _ is the date when the 105th Congress convened. (*1997*)

11. President John Adams was born in Quincy _ in 1735. (*Massachusetts*)

67   COMMA: Misuses (35h)

Cross out all misused commas in the following paragraphs.

Example: Aquifers can be recharged by rainfall, but, the process is slow.
Aquifers can be recharged by rainfall, but/ the process is slow.

An important source of water~~,~~ is underground aquifers. These are deep~~,~~ and sometimes huge layers of water~~,~~ that are trapped between layers of rock. The water is contained in porous rock~~,~~ or in sediment. Deep wells are drilled through the top layers of impervious rock~~,~~ and produce a flow of water. The wells are sometimes called~~,~~ artesian wells.

One of the largest aquifers in North America is~~,~~ the Ogallala aquifer, named after the Indian tribe~~,~~ that once lived in the region~~,~~ and hunted buffalo there. It underlies the western portion of Texas through northern Nebraska, and has a huge capacity of fresh water~~,~~ that is contained in a layer of sand and gravel.

But~~,~~ the water is being removed at a rate faster than it is being replaced. Water is pumped for many purposes such as~~,~~ drinking and other household use, industrial use, and~~,~~ agricultural use. The Great Plains area above the Ogallala~~,~~ often has insufficient rainfall for the crops~~,~~ that are grown there. As a consequence, the crops are watered by irrigation systems~~,~~ that pump water from the Ogallala~~,~~ and distribute it from half-mile-long arms.

Scientists estimate that~~,~~ at the present rate of consumption the Ogallala will be depleted in forty years. They estimate further~~,~~ that water table levels are receding from six inches to three feet a year, depending on location. Some areas are experiencing water shortages already, and the pumping continues.

Federal regulation might make water conservation more likely. Without conservation, the Ogallala will~~,~~ one day~~,~~ be depleted.

68   COMMA: Review (35)

Add commas to the following paragraphs where they are needed, and cross out the ones that are not needed.

Example:
Oak trees have the generic name, *Quercus* and the live oak's name is *Quercus virginiana.*
Oak trees have the generic name~~,~~ Quercus, and the live oak's name is Quercus virginiana.

People~~,~~ who are accustomed to seeing only the red oaks common to the northern United States, will be quite surprised at the appearance of the live oak tree. A type of red oak, the live oak is common only to the coastal region of the deep South.

The live oak tree may be slightly shorter than other oaks~~,~~ classified as red oaks, but it is magnificently broader. It may grow as tall as forty to fifty feet with a trunk diameter of three to four feet. The trunk is short~~,~~ but the tree has a wide-spreading crown. A live oak in the courtyard of the Alamo in San Antonio, Texas, spreads out over the entire area. Its long, heavy limbs are supported with forked posts driven into the ground.

One feature that makes the live oak very different from northern oaks is that it is evergreen. Anyone~~,~~ who has raked leaves in the fall~~,~~ can appreciate the fact~~,~~ that there is no time when the live oak drops all its oval, evergreen leaves. Even though hardly anyone would miss the raking, a person used to the red, gold, and brown colors~~,~~ of fall would surely have a twinge of longing for the deciduous trees of the north.

Squirrels might prefer the live oak to the northern oaks for two reasons. The first is that the dark, ellipsoidal acorns of the live oak are not bitter, whereas those of the northern red oaks are so bitter that even hungry squirrels shun them. The second reason squirrels might prefer the live oaks is that, unlike other red oaks, these trees grow their acorns in one season. In this shorter maturation time, they are more like the trees classified as white oaks.

Other types of live oaks grow on the West Coast, and other types of evergreen oaks can be found in areas of the South.

69   SEMICOLON (36)

The following sentences are correct as written. Write sentences of your own that match the given sentences in linking main clauses (with semicolon alone or with semicolon and conjunctive adverb or transitional expression) or in separating main clauses or series items that contain commas.

Example: Some cities have enacted noise laws; however, enforcement is difficult.
Some people don't watch television; however, bad programs survive.

1. Noise has many definitions; a familiar one calls it unwanted sound.

2. Excessive noise has a number of undesirable effects on people; among them are hypertension, vertigo, stomach ulcers, and allergies.

3. Noise might be regarded as a type of pollution in our industrial society; sound levels seem to increase with population.

4. Mechanical devices such as lawn mowers, automobiles, and airplanes are causes of much of the noise; and amplification of sound devices such as radios, stereos, and rock concerts are further contributors.

5. People's tolerance and preferences for sound vary; for example, some people like to play their stereos loud enough to feel the beat, while others like their music in the background.

6. Some people spending a day on the water prefer the noise, speed, and maneuverability of personal watercraft; however, others want to hear the birds and the gentle lap of the water.

7. Many people experience hearing impairment; the most common cause is continued exposure to loud noise.

8. People who work in noisy environments are at risk of hearing loss; however, the hearing loss from infrequent exposure is likely to be temporary.

9. The long-term effects of exposure to excessive noise may be total loss of hearing; therefore, a person is wise to protect the ears.

70 SEMICOLON: Misuses (36d)

Cross out each unneeded semicolon in the following paragraphs, and substitute any other punctuation mark that may be needed instead.

Example: Vampire bats live about nine years in the wild~~;~~, although their life spans may be expanded to twenty years in captivity.

As a result of its depiction in horror films and novels~~;~~, the vampire bat has a decidedly unsavory reputation as a parasitic creature that attacks human beings and sucks their blood. The truth is~~;~~, unfortunately, it does feed on the blood of animals. While its connection with a certain night-stalking human in a black cape is purely fictional~~;~~, it does indeed thrive on a nightly meal of blood.

The preferred meal of the vampire bat is the blood of domestic animals such as~~;~~ cows, pigs, horses, and sometimes turkeys and chickens. However, it has also been known to feed on sleeping humans. With its long, sharp incisor teeth, it slashes open the skin of its prey; then, with a specially adapted tongue, it laps up the blood that flows from the wound. The bat has chemicals in its saliva that prevent blood from clotting while the bat feeds.

Although there is no danger of a person turning into a vampire from the bite of the bat~~;~~, there is a real risk of rabies. Livestock owners in affected areas often inject their cattle with anticoagulants~~;~~ that cause internal bleeding in the bats. If the bat is not carrying rabies or other diseases~~;~~, there is usually no ill effect on the animal it attacks~~;~~, although sometimes, when several bats feed together, the animal is seriously weakened.

Vampire bats are about the size of mice and, true to their reputation, sleep upside down during the day in caves or hollow trees. They live in colonies that usually number about 100~~;~~, but may amount to as many as 2000. Their range is Central and South America including Mexico but not the southern tip of Argentina.

71 COLON (37)

At each _ mark, decide whether the sentence requires a colon. If it does, add the colon above the insertion mark.

Example: The Russian empress Catherine the Great wrote in several genres : comedies, memoirs, and stories.

The Hermitage in Saint Petersburg, Russia, is one of the world's foremost museums of art. It contains _ the art of many civilizations and artists. Among the masters represented are : Rembrandt, Leonardo da Vinci, Raphael, and El Greco. It also has a large collection of works from more modern painters such as _ Paul Cezanne, Pablo Picasso, and Claude Monet. Numerous countries are represented, including _ Spain, France, Italy, and the Netherlands. In addition to paintings, the museum has collections in other art forms : tapestries, coins, silver, furniture, and armor.

The Hermitage buildings themselves are worthy of note. The original building was reconstructed in neoclassical style from the palace of Catherine II, who ruled Russia from 1762 to 1796. A patron of the arts and literature, Catherine dedicated the palace as a museum and made generous contributions to its collections. The Hermitage Museum now consists of : the Great Hermitage, the Little Hermitage, the New Hermitage, and the Winter Palace. Significant portions of the museum are _ a tribute to Peter I (Peter the Great) and a War Museum.

Catherine instituted the Hermitage as the museum of the Russian imperial family, and, even though it was opened to the public in 1852, for many years it contained only the imperial collections. But with the October Revolution of 1917, collections were confiscated from private owners and added to the museum. Today visitors from all over the world travel to Saint Petersburg _ to view its impressive collections.

72 APOSTROPHE: Possessive case (38a)

Change every underlined word in sentences 1-5 from singular to plural. Adjust apostrophes as required by the changes.

   Example: The mammoth's nature, like the elephant's, was probably sociable.
   The mammoths' nature, like the elephants', was probably sociable.

1. The elephant's prehistoric ancestor was the mammoth.

2. On an animal slightly larger than the elephant, the mammoth's tusks were much longer.

3. The scientist's best guess is that the mammoth lived 2 million years ago.

4. The archaeologist's discovery of deep-frozen whole mammoths in the Arctic tundra has provided useful information about the animal.

5. The mammoth's diet was herbivorous, like the elephant's.

Change every underlined word in sentences 6-10 from plural to singular. Adjust apostrophes as required by the changes.

   Example: Because of a similar diet, the mammoths' and elephants' teeth are very much alike.
   Because of a similar diet, the mammoth's and elephant's teeth are very much alike.

6. The mammoths' Arctic habitat made their long thick coats necessary.

7. Another way their appearance was different from the elephants' appearance was that the mammoths' ears were much smaller.

8. This difference was another of the northern climates' influences, smaller ears being less likely to freeze.

9. The mammoths' primary enemy was humans, who hunted them with spears and axes.

10. The saber-toothed tigers' preying on the mammoths' young would also have decreased the herds' sizes.

73 APOSTROPHE: Contractions (38c)

Underline the correct contraction from the choices given in brackets.

Example: New pets [*are'nt*, <u>*aren't*</u>] always acceptable to roommates.

Nick and Juan shared an apartment in student-housing near [*there, their, they're*] college. They were both expecting to graduate in the class of [*'03, 03, 03'*]. The two roommates [*didn't, did'nt*] have many problems getting along together because [*they're, their, there*] personalities [*were'nt, weren't*] very different. They agreed on which jobs were [*who's, whose*]: Nick did the cooking, and Juan did the cleaning. Nick [*was'nt, wasn't, wasnt*] a smoker, and neither was Juan. They were good friends.

But one day Nick brought home a new pet: a white-furred, pink-eyed ferret. *[He'd, hed]* seen it at the pet store and [*could'nt, couldn't*] resist buying it and bringing it home. What he [*didn't, didnt, did'nt*] buy was a cage to keep the ferret in. He thought he could just let it run around the apartment. Juan thought otherwise.

"[*Whose, Who's*] going to clean up after that thing?" he asked Nick as they both watched the ferret run across a chair, jump onto the stereo, and glare down at them. "[*Its, It's*] going to be making messes all over the place."

"Oh, he [*won't, wont, wo'nt*] be any problem," said Nick. "[*I'll, Il'l, Ill*] have him trained in no time. The salesperson at the store says [*they're, their, there*] very intelligent and learn fast."

Just then the ferret jumped down from the stereo, raced across the floor, and ran straight up one of the draperies. Eying [*its, it's*] position at the top of the drape, Juan told his roommate, "I [*don't do'nt, don't*] know about that. This could be the end of a perfect friendship."

"Well," replied Nick, "maybe we can give the little guy a week and see if he works out. I can take him back if he [*does'nt, doesn't, doesnt*]."

74 APOSTROPHES (38)

Add apostrophes to the underlined words wherever required by convention. If no apostrophe is required, write OK. If you encounter a case in which the apostrophe is optional, write Optional.

Example: The <u>Smiths</u> daughter collects 8-track tapes. → Smiths'

1. During the <u>1970s,</u> <u>Americans</u> could choose from either 8-track tapes or cassette tapes.

2. Although <u>thousands</u> of people owned 8-track tape players, cassette tapes gradually won the market.

3. Many music <u>lovers</u> <u>cars</u> began to feature cassette <u>players</u>.

4. A group of <u>collectors</u> still searches for 8-track tapes in yard <u>sales</u>.

5. More recently, <u>CDs</u> have begun to replace cassette tapes as the format of choice.

6. A CD is more durable than a cassette tape—as long as you avoid scratching <u>its</u> surface.

7. Compared to a cassette <u>tapes</u> quality, a <u>CDs</u> quality is generally regarded as superior.

8. Many music <u>lovers</u> actually prefer the grainy sound of vinyl records on their <u>stereos</u>.

9. The <u>scratches</u> and other imperfections are music to a record <u>collectors</u> ears.

10. Usually a turntable must be purchased separately, since most sound <u>systems</u> today do not include one.

75 APOSTROPHE: Review (38)

Add apostrophes to the underlined words wherever required by convention.

Example: Many of <u>Londons</u> **London's** <u>churches</u> were designed by famous <u>architects</u>.

1. One place that <u>tourists</u> to England often visit is <u>Britains</u> Westminster Abbey.

2. The <u>abbeys</u> actual name is <u>Londons</u> Collegiate Church of Saint Peter in Westminster.

3. <u>Its</u> the place where <u>Englands</u> <u>kings</u> and <u>queens</u> are crowned.

4. Royalty are also married there, and noted <u>poets</u> Geoffrey Chaucer and Robert Browning are buried in <u>Poets</u> Corner.

5. The church was originally a Norman church, but Henry III demolished it in 1245 and began a new structure that would take <u>centuries</u> to complete.

6. The <u>transepts</u> and part of the nave were finished in only three <u>years</u> time, but the remainder took many more <u>years</u> for completion.

7. The nave was not completed until the sixteenth century, and <u>Henry VIIIs</u> Lady Chapel was finished at about that same time.

8. The western <u>towers</u> were Christopher <u>Wrens</u> and Nicholas <u>Hawksmoors</u> <u>contributions</u>.

9. These noted <u>architects</u> are responsible for some of <u>its</u> fame as a historic monument.

10. Wren also designed many of <u>Londons</u> other <u>churches</u>; <u>its</u> St. <u>Pauls</u> Cathedral for which <u>hes</u> best known.

11. Hawksmoor also designed many churches and assisted Wren in St. Pauls design.

12. The designs of many of Englands baroque buildings are his.

13. Westminister Abbeys design bears some similarity to Chartres Cathedrals design.

14. The abbey is famous for its architecture, but its the historic significance that draws many tourists.

76   PUNCTUATION REVIEW: Apostrophes and Hyphens (38, 42)

Revise the use of apostrophes and hyphens as needed in the following passage. In some cases, you may have to add an apostrophe or hyphen; in others, you may have to delete an apostrophe or hyphen.

Example: The library shows childrens movies after school.

Answer: The library shows children's movies after school.

The environment a child grows up in has an effect on the childs entire life. According to *Raising Children in the United States*, in more than two thirds of American households, both parent's work outside the home, and children are housed in daycare centers. The premise of the book is that couples who are considering having children should consider the need for stay at home parenting. Would be parents must consider the need to forsake careers and devote their time to their new infants. Parent's want their children to develop a good self concept or proper self esteem. Parents want their children to feel the security that evolve's from growing up in a strong, supportive family. Support from a family is essential to the childrens mental development, happiness, and contentment. Thus, its worthwhile to make sacrifices in order to see that children have a bright future. The reward is raising a secure individual with a sense of self worth.

77   QUOTATION MARKS I (39)

Rewrite each of the following indirect quotations as direct quotations, placing quotation marks where it seems the quotation begins and ends. Position quotation marks appropriately in relation to other marks. You may have to change some words that introduce the quotation.

Example: Some of the things we do, according to the poet Horace, seem as crazy as hauling timber into the woods.
"Some of the things we do," according to the poet Horace, "seem as crazy as hauling timber into the woods."

1. The Roman poet Horace was probably the first to use the Latin phrase *carpe diem*, telling us to seize the day!

2. Of course, he is also known to have advised that life grants nothing to us mortals without hard work.

3. He who has begun has half done, Horace reminds us further. He says to dare to be wise and begin!

4. Then, if you take his advice and work hard to achieve the heights of success, he warns that it is the mountaintop that the lightning strikes.

5. Horace also has advice for beginning writers, reminding us that even old Homer nods.

6. He may have been the first to advise against the use of foot-and-a-half long words.

7. He characterized the difficulty of writing when he said that the mountains will be in labor, and a ridiculous mouse will be brought forth.

8. He was probably recalling that Aesop had also written that a tiny mouse came out of a great mountain.

9. Regarding speech, Horace declares that once a word has been allowed to escape, it cannot be recalled.

10. Horace also points out the benefits of social responsibility when he says that it is your concern when your neighbor's wall is on fire.

78 QUOTATION MARKS OR UNDERLINING (39, 44a)

The passage below contains a number of titles. Punctuate each title with either quotation marks or underlining (italics).

Example: Sangster's poem Awakening reminds the reader that spring always comes.

Answer: Sangster's poem "Awakening" reminds the reader that spring always comes.

The introductory chapter of Elizabeth Wurtzel's book is called Manufacturing Fascination. She argues that people are fascinated with "women of great mischief," and points to numerous magazine articles, such as one in Elle called The Rise and Rise of the Bad Girl. She also appreciates the attention given to "dangerous women" in an issue of Esquire, which showed on its cover a photograph of the pinup girl for the Third Reich and the headline I'm Sorry I Ruined Your Life. Cosmopolitan, Wurtzel points out, covered the subject of certain difficult women in an article called Hollywood Brats. And Allure picked up on the subject of celebrities acting out their anger, in Temper, Temper. Wurtzel even cites Trish Yearwood and her song I Want to Go Too Far as evidence that being bad can feel good. As another example from the world of music, she cites You Oughta Know, the hit song by Alanis Morisette that illustrates how a woman can achieve dignity through anger over betrayal.

79 QUOTATION MARKS II (39)

Correct any uses of double quotation marks, single quotation marks, and adjacent punctuation in the following sentences. If no correction is needed, write OK.

Example: According to Jane Bryant Quinn, "Pawnshops and shops advertising "loans until payday" are sprouting in the suburbs."

Answer: According to Jane Bryant Quinn, "Pawnshops and shops advertising 'loans until payday' are sprouting in the suburbs."

1. One suburban mother of three said, "I never thought I'd be standing in front of a pawnbroker, asking 'How much can you give me for this'?"

2. "I go to the local pawnbroker when I need a little more money before payday" said a secretary we interviewed.

3. Who knows how many wedding rings have been pawned for "just a few days?"

4. Several strip malls in town now offer "loans until payday."

5. "Unlike old-fashioned pawnshops" explains one manager "modern ones sell everything from wedding rings to CD players."

6. "I don't think pawnshops are a 'get rich quick' proposition," he warned.

7. Unlike conventional pawnbrokers, Jack Swanson specializes in expensive and 'one of a kind' jewelry.

8. Many of his clients—both buyers and sellers—tell him that "I never thought I'd be standing in a pawnshop".

9. "One customer told me, 'I've never bought a piece of jewelry at anywhere but Tiffany's,'" said Swanson.

10. "Some of my best customers start out selling me their jewelry and then come back later to buy other people's"! exclaimed Swanson.

80   DASH, PARENTHEES, ELLIPSIS MARK, BRACKETS, SLASH (40)

As appropriate, insert at each _ mark a dash, parenthesis, ellipsis mark, bracket, or slash. If no punctuation is needed, leave the space blank.

Example: Twain, accounting for his pen name, wrote, "I confiscated the ancient

   ( )
mariner's discarded one _ 'Mark Twain'_ ."

1. Poet and editor Margaret Elizabeth Sangster _ 1838-1912 _ wrote the lines, "Never yet was a springtime, _ Late though lingered the snow, _ That the sap stirred not at the whisper _ Of the southwind, sweet and low; _ Never yet was a springtime _ When the buds forgot to blow."

2. In the term paper, her poem _ "Awakening" _ was quoted in shortened form: "Never yet was a springtime, _ When the buds forgot to blow."

3. On one level, Sangster's poem reminds the reader that spring always comes _ "Late though linger_s_ the snow."

4. On another level, she tells the reader that troubles will end, and, with a gentle nudge _ when "the sap stirred _ at the whisper" _ life will be good again.

5. In a speech _ "To the Young People's Society," delivered at Greenpoint Presbyterian Church, Brooklyn _ February 16, 1901_ _ , Mark Twain advised his audience, "Always do right. This will gratify some people, and astonish the rest."_

6. The advice of Twain _ Samuel Langhorne Clemens _ seems to imply that in general people don't expect good behavior from young people, that such behavior might "astonish" them.

7. However, he does say that when young people "do right," "_ t_his will gratify some people."

81 PUNCTUATION REVIEW (34-40)

Insert appropriate punctuation above the _ marks. If no punctuation is needed, leave the space blank.

Example: The basic rules of etiquette _ remain the same over time _**:**_ be thoughtful of those around you.

When it comes to socializing _ the rules and guidelines sometimes change over the years _ and sometimes remain the same. Amy Vanderbilt_s guide to etiquette published in 1952 _ has suggestions for smoking _ that are generally not applicable today _ however _ her guidelines for what to do when we can _ t remember names are helpful at any time.

Regarding smoking _ Vanderbilt advises the considerate man _ whether a smoker or not _ to carry a lighter so that he will be prepared when a _ lady _ takes out a cigarette and looks as if she_s expecting a light. The rules concerning inappropriate times to smoke reflect the regulations of an earlier era too. People are advised not to smoke in buses _ churches _ or elevators _ for example_ It is likewise inappropriate _ according to Vanderbilt _ to visit a newborn baby with a cigar _ or cigarette in hand.

But the matter of remembering names has changed little. Most people _ who have encountered a familiar person and can_t recall the name _ can profit from Vanderbilt_s sensible suggestions. She advises avoiding the trite _ I know your face but can_t recall the name_ _ Instead _ you can say something like _ Nice to see you _ _ and let the other person do the talking_ to perhaps give you a clue about the name. Just hope the person doesn't say _ _

Do you remember me _ _ To prevent the awkwardness of these situations _ Vanderbilt advises _ that _ upon meeting someone _ whom we see infrequently _ we say something like _ _ How do you do_ I_m John Doe_ We met at the student government meeting last fall _ _ In other words_ we can assume_ that the other person is having the same trouble remembering a name.

82 SPELLING: Typical problems I (41a)

From the options given in brackets, underline the spelling that is correct in the context of each sentence.

Example: Air pollution [*affects*, *effects*] everyone's health to some extent.

1. Unless Ed learns to [*curb*, *curve*] his temper, he'll be fired.

2. As soon as the chairperson restored order to the meeting, we [*preceded*, *proceeded*] with the discussion.

3. The movie was [*adapted*, *adopted*] from a short story.

4. Some of the manufacturing [*personal*, *personnel*] were warned that the facility where they worked would soon be sold.

5. The new president of the university will be [*formally*, *formerly*] inducted into office next week.

6. A showdown between the two opponents is [*eminent*, *imminent*].

7. A mirage is an optical [*allusion*, *illusion*] caused by atmospheric conditions.

8. The [*principal*, *principle*] reason he got elected was the amount of money he spent on advertising.

9. According to the [*eminent*, *imminent*] bacteriologist Dr. Morgan Furthwold, the laboratory is on the verge of a breakthrough.

10. The surveys were mailed [*to*, *too*, *two*] late for some people to respond.

83 SPELLING: Typical problems II (41a)

From the options given in brackets, underline the spelling that is correct in the context of each sentence.

Example: The representative from student government made her [*presence*, *presents*] known quietly but assertively.

1. The sign in the store drew attention to the [*stationary, stationery*] envelopes.

2. The kitten was amusing itself on the rug by chasing [*it's, its*] tail.

3. The yellow mustang convertible [*passed, past*] us at a high rate of speed.

4. When registering for classes, [*your, you're*] likely to have some problems meeting [*your, you're*] requirements.

5. Many people are not knowledgeable about how [*their, there, they're*] actions can [*affect, effect*] the environment.

6. For the [*forth, fourth*] time that morning, Allen tried to get through on the Internet.

7. Sylvia made an appointment at the placement office to get some [*advice, advise*] on her career.

8. Many [*woman, women*] in business still report encountering a glass ceiling that hinders their advancement.

9. I had [*all ready, already*] read the chapter when it was assigned.

10. Some people find it very difficult to [*accept, except*] a compliment graciously.

11. Because there was no name on the failing paper, the instructor didn't know [*who's, whose*] it was, and nobody would claim it.

12. Our family has traced our [*decent, descent*] to Irish refugees in the eighteenth century.

13. The fraternity house was warned that any future [*incidence, incidents*] would result in disciplinary action.

84   SPELLING: Rules (41b)

In the space above each word, practice the appropriate spelling rule for each group.

1. Insert *ie* or *ei* as appropriate:

   a. bel____ve   d. rec____ve   g. h____ght

   b. perc____ve   e. rel____ve   h. hyg____ne

   c. ____ght   f. b____ge   i. th____f

2. Drop the final *-e* or keep it:

   a. knowledge + able   d. notice + able   g. recognize + able

   b. love + ing   e. notice + ed   h. imagine + ation

   c. change + able   f. pursue + ant   i. imagine + ing

3. Change the final *-y* to *-i* or keep it:

   a. happy + ly   d. study + ing   g. physiology + cal

   b. forty + ish   e. study + s   h. supply + ed

   c. hypocrisy + s   f. Barry + s   i. buy + s

4. Double the final consonant or not:

   a. stop + ed   d. defer + ment   g. occur + ence

   b. prefer + ed   e. refer + ence   h. travel + ed

   c. begin + ing   f. permit + ed   i. benefit + ing

5. Write the correct plural:

   a. woman   d. analysis   g. phenomenon

   b. thesis   e. deer   h. crisis

   c. datum   f. potato   i. criterion

85   HYPHEN (42)

Insert hyphens wherever they are needed at the _ marks.

Example: Elephants have twelve_inch_long teeth, but they have only four of them.
Elephants have twelve-inch-long teeth, but they have only four of them.

1. The African elephant is well-known for its size.

2. A male elephant might weigh five and one-half to six tons, and a female might weigh up to four tons.

3. Both male and female elephants might grow to a ten-foot height.

4. The non-African elephants of south-central Asia are somewhat smaller.

5. The fourteen- or fifteen-year-old elephant has reached sexual maturity.

6. The elephant life span is about sixty-five or seventy years.

7. A newborn elephant calf weighs two- to three-hundred pounds.

8. It stands about thirty-three inches high.

9. A two-hundred-pound, thirty-three-inch-tall baby is quite a big baby.

10. Elephants live together in family units, although the adult male is solitary.

11. Elephants are vegetarians and can eat up to five hundred pounds of food a day.

12. Unfortunately, African elephants are endangered, and poaching for their tusks is widespread.

13. Governmental efforts in African nations have made it illegal to sell ivory and elephant tusks.

86   CAPITAL LETTERS I (43)

Capitalize words in the following paragraphs as required by convention.

> *Example:*   in preparing to write his paper, frederick read background information, literary criticisms, and the literature itself.
> In preparing to write his paper, Frederick read background information, literary criticisms, and the literature itself.

frederick decided to write a paper for his honors english class that explored the history of literature in the harlem renaissance. his instructor, professor packer, suggested a few places where frederick might start looking. first he read the entry titled "harlem renaissance" in *collier's encyclopedia*. then he found a book entitled *harlem renaissance*, and that gave him even more background. at the back of the book was a bibliography that gave him some more titles to search for. from there he searched his library and the internet.

he found information on the period of the harlem renaissance itself, sometimes called the "decade of the new negro," a period spanning 1917 to 1935. it was a time when african-american arts and literature flourished in the harlem district of new york city. the word *renaissance* itself means "rebirth," and the period was characterized by a new interest in the heritage of african americans.

frederick also learned about some influential leaders among the african americans of the era. they were w. e. b. dubois, james weldon johnson, and marcus garvey. frederick read about their ideologies and began to understand how they differed from one another. then he began concentrating on the literature of the period. jean toomer was the author he started with. he read toomer's novel *cane* and appreciated its style and structure. he especially enjoyed reading the first part, which consists of six short stories about six georgian women--five african-american and one white.

the paper that frederick finally wrote examined the work of countee cullen and langston hughes as well as that of toomer.

87 CAPITAL LETTERS II (43)

Correct any errors in capitalization in the following sentences. If there are no errors, mark the sentence as "Correct."

Example: Many cities reflect earlier stages in American ~~History~~ history.

1. San Diego is a city of many cultures.

2. Because the Mexican border is so close by, Mexican culture can be noticed in the street signs (e.g., el camino real), the town names (La jolla), and the architecture.

3. Many immigrants from Laos, cambodia, and vietnam have settled in this city.

4. As a result, it is not uncommon to find vietnamese restaurants dotting the streets throughout the city.

5. Local schools teach many students whose first language is not english.

6. At Crawford junior high, there is a center for "newcomers."

7. Students can learn about American Culture and the English Language at this center.

8. On may 5 of every year, many San Diegans celebrate the victory of the mexican battle against the french.

9. This celebration is a time for dancing, eating, and drinking, especially in Old Town, the historical part of the City.

10. The Ethnic diversity of the city is a source of richness for inhabitants and visitors alike.

88 UNDERLINING or ITALICS I (44)

Underline all words in the following sentences that should be underlined or italicized to accord with convention.

Example: Kenneth Burke applied the term <u>dramatism</u> to his discussion of rhetoric.

1. The word <u>rhetoric</u> has many meanings, some of them distinctly uncomplimentary.

2. One of the oldest comes from Aristotle in his book <u>Rhetoric</u>.

3. Aristotle defined rhetoric as "the faculty of observing in any given case the available means of persuasion."

4. The Greek words <u>ethos</u>, <u>pathos</u>, and <u>logos</u> represent the three modes of persuasion that Aristotle identified.

5. Another Greek philosopher, Plato, defined rhetoric not so much as persuasion as a seeking after truth.

6. In his <u>Phaedrus</u>, Plato shows how truth can be worked out through dialogues.

7. He concentrates more on <u>logos</u>, or the appeal of reason, than on <u>ethos</u> and <u>pathos</u>, the appeals of character and emotion.

8. A Roman rhetorician, Quintilian, in his <u>Institutes of Oratory</u>, focused more on ethos, saying that it is essential for the speaker or writer to be a good person.

9. Twentieth-century rhetorician Kenneth Burke wrote a number of books on rhetoric, among them these two: <u>A Grammar of Motives</u> and <u>A Rhetoric of Motives</u>.

10. In these books, as well as in another, <u>Counter-Statement</u>, Burke takes the position that all discourse is persuasive and therefore rhetorical.

11. Another twentieth-century writer, Wayne Booth, in <u>The Rhetoric of Fiction</u>, defined the word <u>rhetoric</u> almost as widely as Burke did.

89   UNDERLINING OR ITALICS II (44)

Underline all words in the following sentences that should be underlined or italicized to accord with convention. If no changes are needed, write OK.

Example: In <u>The Right Stuff</u>, Tom Wolfe writes about the first Americans in space.

1. In 1986, the space shuttle <u>Challenger</u> exploded shortly after liftoff, killing Christa McAuliffe.

2. On February 1, 2003, the shuttle <u>Columbia</u> disintegrated as it was re-entering the earth's atmosphere.

3. The stress of re-entry was portrayed in the movie <u>Apollo 13</u>.

4. Viewers at Cape Canaveral were expecting an uneventful landing because of the perfect weather conditions.

5. A special report in <u>Newsweek</u> included profiles of the seven astronauts who were killed.

6. One of the astronauts, Kalpana Chawla, had reported that the Nile River "looks like a lifeline in the Sahara" when viewed from space.

7. Astronaut John Glenn, the first American to orbit the Earth, explained that the <u>Columbia</u> tragedy was the first time a disaster had occurred on re-entry.

8. The associate director of the California Space Institute speculated that funding problems may be at the root of the disaster.

9. Several commentators appeared on the <u>Today</u> show during the week following the accident.

10. Homeland Security officials did not believe that terrorism was involved.

90   ABBREVIATIONS I (45)

Revise these sentences to spell out any abbreviations that are not appropriate for nontechnical writing.

Example: The term *dreadnought* referring to heavily armed battleships has not been used since early in the 20th cent.
twentieth century.

1. The H.M.S. *Dreadnought* was a battleship launched in 1906 as the first of its type.

2. Smaller arms were dispensed with to make room for larger guns such as its ten 12-in. guns in five armored turrets.

3. It also had 11-in.-thick armor to guard against torpedoes.

4. It had a max. speed of 21 kn., which was faster than the speed of most other battleships.

5. The ship, built for the Brit. navy, was completed in only one yr.

6. So popular was this ship for its time that the term *dreadnought* came to refer to any heavily armed and heavily armored warship before and during the 1st World War.

7. Still larger vessels used during W.W.I. were called *superdreadnoughts*.

8. The British *Queen Eliz.* could travel through the water at about 25 kn.

9. It had eight 15-in. guns and displaced 33,000 tons.

10. The largest battleship ever built was the *Yamato*, which had a max. speed of 27 kn. and displaced nearly 73,000 tns.

11. The *Yamato* was a Japanese ship built during the 2nd World War.

12. US battleships were decommissioned in 1958, but a few were recommissioned again in 1981.

13. Battleships of the US, U.K., and other countries are no longer referred to by the menacing term *dreadnought*.

91 ABBREVIATIONS II (45)

Revise the following sentences to spell out any abbreviations that are not appropriate for nontechnical writing or to correct any improperly punctuated abbreviations. Write OK if the abbreviation is correct.

PH.D.   **OK**

Example: A PhD is the terminal (i.e., highest) degree in many academic fields.

Bob Berger, MD, holds a degree in pharmacology and biochemistry. Dr. Berger researches and develops products to improve people's health. He is also a co-owner of a special vitamin store located in So. Fl. The store is located on Fed. Hwy., not far from Airline Blvd. Berger works long hrs. at the store counseling people with health problems. From Mon. to Sat., Bob works from 10 am to at least 6 p.m. Sometimes he stays late or comes in early to do research. He looks for new information on new developments, eg pain-relieving supplements. Berger feels that although conventional medications are good for some people, they may not be good for all people. He is so knowledgeable that he is in demand as a speaker in many cities across the U.S., such as LA, NY, and Washington, D.C. This gifted man is also an author. He helps write the store's monthly newsletter with a special section that is usually on pg. 2. In addition to all of these things, he and his partners own a co. where they make some of the special supplements they sell. As a matter of fact, he has developed an anti-aging product that has become very popular. At 95 dol. per bottle, it's expensive.

92   NUMBERS I (46)

From the choices in brackets, underline the numerals or words that are appropriate for nontechnical writing.

    Example: The Gallipoli Campaign finally ended on [*January 8-9*, the 8th and 9th of January],1915.

1. Gallipoli is a peninsula about [*50*, fifty] miles long in western Turkey.

2. Because of its strategic location at the Dardanelles–a [*40*, forty]-mile-long strait providing access to the Black Sea, Constantinople, and Russia–the peninsula has been the site of many battles.

3. One of those conflicts took place during World War [One, *I*] between the Allied Forces and the Turks, who were fighting on the side of Germany.

4. On February [*19th*, 19, nineteenth], 1915, the British and French together began a naval campaign intended to reduce the Turkish fortifications.

5. The main thrust of the campaign began on March [*18*, 18th, eighteenth] with [*16*, sixteen] battleships providing the firepower.

6. That battle ended with the Turks nearly out of ammunition, but the Allies had lost [*3*, three] battleships to mines and had [*3*, three] others disabled.

7. So the Allies decided on a land campaign, assembling a force of [*78,000*, seventy-eight thousand] men from England, Australia, and New Zealand.

8. The French also drew together a sizable force, and [*thousands*, 1000s] of troops were in place on [*April 24*, the 24th of April].

9. Unfortunately, the Allies were badly organized and not well coordinated, so the Turks had plenty of opportunity to gather a fighting force of [*60,000*, sixty thousand] and to replenish their ammunition.

10. As anyone knows who has watched the movie *Gallipoli*, the battle was a disaster, with casualties as high as [*252,000*, two hundred fifty thousand] for the Allies and nearly as high for the Turks.

93 NUMBERS II (46)

Correct any instances where numerals are used incorrectly, or where numerals need to be used instead of words for numbers. Assume a nontechnical academic writing style. If the use is correct, write OK.

Example: We visited three churches during our 1ˢᵗ day in Florence, Italy.
                                     OK   first

Can you imagine a man who spent 50 years of his life making 4 doors for a building? That is what a man named Lorenzo Ghiberti did in the 15ᵗʰ century to a religious building in Florence, Italy. The doors, which still serve as the entrances to the building, aren't made of wood but are bronze. This is one of the reasons that Ghiberti took five decades to finish them. Another reason for taking so long to complete the work is that the first 2 doors each have 28 different panels. There is a different religious scene on every panel. These pictures are done in a process called *relief*, which means that the pictures are raised above the surface of the door, sort of like flattened-out sculptures. Also, when Ghiberti made each picture, he set it within a frame that is almost as complex as the picture. After working for 21 years to finish these two doors, he began a 2ⁿᵈ set of doors that are often called the *Gates of Paradise*. Each of these doors has 10 large panels, showing scenes from the Christian Bible. In all, the two projects lasted from 1403 to about 1453—a long time to work on four doors for a building.

94   NUMBERS III (46)

Correct any instances where numerals are used incorrectly, or where numerals need to be used instead of words for numbers. Assume a technical academic writing style. If the use is correct, write OK.

Example: Our local electronics store carries ~~7~~ **seven** brands of high-definition TVs.

1. Only five years ago, people were predicting the rapid growth of high-definition TV (HDTV).

2. In a regular television broadcast, the picture consists of 480 scan lines.

3. HDTV images contain more scan lines, either seven hundred-twenty or one thousand-eighty.

4. This means that HDTV offers 2 times the resolution of regular TV.

5. While traditional televisions have a 4:3 screen ratio, HD sets offer a widescreen format.

6. Regular TVs are not usually larger than thirty-two inches.

7. Some LCD TVs are ten inches larger.

8. Currently, 5 TV technologies are available.

9. All 3 major networks currently offer prime-time shows in HD.

10. By 2006, all TV broadcasts may be in HD.

95 AVOIDING PLAGIARISM AND DOCUMENTING SOURCES I (50)

The following source material is from page 56 of an article by Ian Parker called "Reading Minds," which appeared on pp. 52-63 of the January 20, 2003 issue of the *New Yorker*: "The locked-in state can be mistaken for a coma, and a coma can be mistaken for a locked-in state. A locked-in diagnosis (the term was first used in 1966 by the American neurologists Jerome Posner and Fred Plum) means that although a person has been abandoned by his or her body, the brain still functions."

Example: Explain whether the following use of the source material is documented correctly or not. Assume the writer is following MLA style.

The term "locked-in state" was first used in 1966 by two American neurologists, Jerome Posner and Fred Plum.

Answer: The information cited is not common knowledge. In addition, the student writer's paraphrase relies heavily on Parker's phrasing, and therefore should not be represented as the work of the student writer. To avoid plagiarism, the student writer should place quotation marks around directly quoted material and attribute the information to Parker.

1. Explain whether the following use of the source material is documented correctly or not. Assume the writer is following MLA style.

According to Parker, a locked-in diagnosis means that although a person has been abandoned by his or her body, the brain still functions (56).

2. Explain whether the following use of the source material is documented correctly or not. Assume the writer is following MLA style.

According to Parker, a locked-in diagnosis means that although a person has been "abandoned by his or her body," the brain still functions (56).

3. Explain whether the following use of the source material is documented correctly or not. Assume the writer is following MLA style.

One source observes that the locked-in state "can be mistaken for a coma," and that a coma "can be mistaken for a locked-in state" (Parker 56).

4. Explain whether the following use of the source material is documented correctly or not. Assume the writer is following MLA style.

A locked-in state means that although a person no longer has control over his or her body, the brain still works (Parker 56).

5. Explain whether the following use of the source material is documented correctly or not. Assume the writer is following MLA style.

According to Parker, "The locked-in state can be mistaken for a coma, and a coma can be mistaken for a locked-in state" (56).

6. Construct an in-text citation for the original quotation using APA style. Use the phrase *According to Parker* to lead into the quotation.

7. Document the source for a list of references using MLA style.

8. Document the source for a list of references using APA style.

9. Document the source for a list of references using Chicago style.

10. Document the source for a list of references using CSE name-year style.

96 AVOIDING PLAGIARISM AND DOCUMENTING SOURCES II (50)

The following source material is from page 54 of an article by Hideko Takayama called "The Okinawa Way," which appeared on pp. 54-55 of the January 13, 2003 issue of *Newsweek*: "Toguchi is one of about 600 centenarians out of a population of 1.3 million. Indeed, Okinawa has the highest proportion of centenarians in the world: 39.5 for every 100,000 people, compared with about 10 in 100,000 Americans."

Example: Explain whether the following use of the source material is documented correctly or not. Assume the writer is following MLA style.

According to Takayama, Okinawa has about 600 centenarians out of a population of 1.3 million (54).

Answer: The information cited is not common knowledge, so the student writer is correct in attributing it to Takayama. However, the student writer's paraphrase relies heavily on Takayama's phrasing, and therefore should not be represented as the work of the student writer. To avoid plagiarism, the student writer should place quotation marks around directly quoted material and attribute the information to Takayama.

1. Explain whether the following use of the source material is documented correctly or not. Assume the writer is following MLA style.

Okinawa has 39.5 centenarians for every 100,000 people.

2. Explain whether the following use of the source material is documented correctly or not. Assume the writer is following MLA style.

According to one source, Okinawa has the highest proportion of centenarians in the world.

3. Explain whether the following use of the source material is documented correctly or not. Assume the writer is following MLA style.

According to one source, Okinawa has the highest proportion of centenarians in the world (54).

4. Explain whether the following use of the source material is documented correctly or not. Assume the writer is following MLA style.

Okinawa has the highest percentage of centenarians in the world: "39.5 for every 100,000 people" (Takayama 54)

5. Explain whether the following use of the source material is documented correctly or not. Assume the writer is following MLA style.

According to one source, "Okinawa has the highest proportion of centenarians in the world: 39.5 for every 100,000 people" (Takayama 54).

6. Construct an in-text citation for the original quotation using APA style. Use the phrase *According to Tagayama* to lead into the quotation.

7. Document the source for a list of references using MLA style.

8. Document the source for a list of references using APA style.

9. Document the source for a list of references using Chicago style.

10. Document the source for a list of references using CSE name-year style.

97 AVOIDING PLAGIARISM AND DOCUMENTING SOURCES: MLA (50, 52)

Document each of the following sources for a list of references using MLA style. You have all the information that you need to prepare each reference, but there may be some information given that you do not need to include.

1. An article by Claudia Rawlins called "Changes in Corporate Culture and Organizational Strategy: The Effect on Technical Writers." The article appeared on pp. 31-35 of volume 15 of *The Technical Writing Teacher* in 1988.

2. An article by Linda Flower, John R. Hayes, Linda Carey, Karen Schriver, and James Stratman called "Detection, Diagnosis, and the Strategies of Revision." The article appeared on pp. 16-55 of volume 37 of *College Composition and Communication* in 1986.

3. The second edition of Thomas Kuhn's book *The Structure of Scientific Revolutions,* which was published in 1970 by the University of Chicago Press in Chicago.

4. An essay by Mary M. Lay called "Gender Studies: Implications for the Professional Communication Classroom." The essay appears on pp. 215-229 of a collection of essays edited by Nancy Roundy Blyler and Charlotte Thralls and published in Newbury Park, California, in 1993 by Sage Publications. The collection is called *Professional Communication: The Social Perspective.*

5. A second essay from the collection described in item (5). This essay is called "Viewing Functional Pictures in Context" and was written by Charles Kostelnick. It appears on pp. 243-256 of the collection. Assume that you are citing both essays in your list of works cited.

6. An entry on "Global warming" found in the 6th edition (2001) of the Columbia Encyclopedia. The source was accessed from http://www.bartleby.com/65/gl/globalwa.html on February 9, 2003. No author is listed for the entry.

7. A message posted to the First Ojibwe Forum 3 bulletin board by Bostjan Dvorak on January 09, 2003 at 09:16:58. The subject line of the message is "Some words." The URL for the forum is http://first-ojibwe.net/. You accessed the message on January 15, 2003.

8. A conference paper called "The chicken, the egg, and African telecommunications," by Barnaby Richards of the University of Colorado at Boulder, delivered at the International Conference on Information Technology, Communications and Development, held in Kathmandu, Nepal on November 29-30, 2001.

9. A newspaper article by Robin Pogrebin called "Showdown over orchestra size looms on Broadway," appearing in the *New York Times* on February 5, 2003. The article starts on p. B1 and continues on p. B3.

10. An article called "Culture" from the Cultural Savvy website at http://www.culturalsavvy.com/culture.htm. The article was accessed on January 31, 2003. No author is listed for the article.

98 AVOIDING PLAGIARISM AND DOCUMENTING SOURCES: APA (50, 53)

Document each of the following sources for a list of references using APA style. You have all the information that you need to prepare each reference, but there may be some information given that you do not need to include.

1. An article by Claudia Rawlins called "Changes in Corporate Culture and Organizational Strategy: The Effect on Technical Writers." The article appeared on pp. 31-35 of volume 15 of *The Technical Writing Teacher* in 1988.

2. An article by Linda Flower, John R. Hayes, Linda Carey, Karen Schriver, and James Stratman called "Detection, Diagnosis, and the Strategies of Revision." The article appeared on pp. 16-55 of volume 37 of *College Composition and Communication* in 1986.

3. The second edition of Thomas Kuhn's book *The Structure of Scientific Revolutions,* which was published in 1970 by the University of Chicago Press in Chicago.

4. An essay by Mary M. Lay called "Gender Studies: Implications for the Professional Communication Classroom." The essay appears on pp. 215-229 of a collection of essays edited by Nancy Roundy Blyler and Charlotte Thralls and published in Newbury Park, California, in 1993 by Sage Publications. The collection is called *Professional Communication: The Social Perspective.*

5. A review of a book called *Presentations in Everyday Life: Strategies for Effective Speaking.* The book is by John A. Daly and Isa N. Engleberg and was published by Houghton Mifflin in 2001. The book review was written by Linda P. Willis and appears on pp. 111-114 of the March 2002 (vol. 65) issue of *Business Communication Quarterly*.

6. An entry on "Global warming" found in the 6th edition (2001) of the Columbia Encyclopedia. The source was accessed from http://www.bartleby.com/65/gl/globalwa.html on February 9, 2003. No author is listed for the entry.

7. A message posted to the First Ojibwe Forum 3 bulletin board by Bostjan Dvorak on January 09, 2003 at 09:16:58. The subject line of the message is "Some words." The URL for the forum is http://first-ojibwe.net/.

8. A government publication by the Immigration and Naturalization Service called *Statistical Yearbook of the Immigration and Naturalization Service*. This item was published in 1993 by the US Government Printing Office.

9. A newspaper article by Robin Pogrebin called "Showdown over orchestra size looms on Broadway," appearing in the *New York Times* on February 5, 2003. The article starts on p. B1 and continues on p. B3.

10. An article called "Culture" from the Cultural Savvy website at http://www.culturalsavvy.com/culture.htm. The article was accessed on January 31, 2003. No author is listed for the article.

99   CRITICALLY VIEWING IMAGES (7b)

Use the strategies outlined in section 7b, "Viewing Images Critically," to discuss the following advertisement. Assume that it is intended to appeal to college students. Remember to consider both visual and textual elements. Organize your discussion around the five strategies of previewing, analyzing, interpreting, synthesizing, and evaluating.

*It's 2 am, your exam is in 6 hours,
your roommate is asleep, and the library is closed*

Need a study partner...

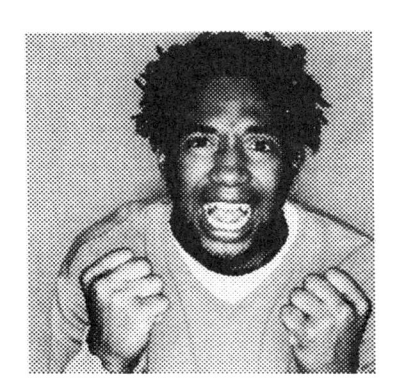

...now?

Don't worry, Longman understands. That's why we're here for you, 24/7. Visit the Companion Website for this text at www.ablongman.com/alexander any time of the day or night. With a wealth of activities, practice tests, links to other helpful sites, chapter summaries, and much more, this study partner is a godsend for the perfectionist and the procrastinator. And the best part? It's FREE.

NOTES

NOTES

NOTES

NOTES